The Coaching Odyssey

The Coaching Odyssey

An Island Tale for Coaches and Leaders
Wanting to Make a Greater Impact

Jennifer Powers

POWERHOUSE PUBLISHING
A Division of Powerhouse Global, Inc.

For all the coaches, all over the world.

Contents

Searching for More

Lucas sat alone in his office, the quiet hum of the city a stark contrast to the turmoil brewing within him. Four years into his coaching career, having left the intensity of the corporate world for what he hoped would be a more fulfilling calling, he found himself at a crossroads. His office, once a symbol of his new beginning, now felt like a gilded cage.

Before making the leap to coaching, Lucas had thrived in the competitive corporate environment, climbing the ranks with a keen insight into organizational dynamics. He had been the go-to person for strategy, known for his ability to navigate complex projects and lead teams to success. But the satisfaction that came from these accomplishments had been fleeting, prompting Lucas to seek a career that touched on deeper transformations.

Coaching had seemed like the answer, a way to leverage his extensive experience to guide others through their professional challenges. Yet, after several years of coaching individuals and consulting for teams, Lucas felt a gnawing emptiness. The tools and action plans he provided his clients with were effective, yet he couldn't shake the feeling that there was more he could offer, a deeper level of impact that lay just beyond his reach.

On this particular evening, Lucas found himself poring over client feedback, the words of praise stark against the glow of his desk lamp. "Insightful," one client had written. "Lucas's strategies are game changers," said another. While gratifying, these accolades echoed the hollow feeling inside him. He wasn't just looking for game-changers; he was searching for life-changers.

The city lights blurred as Lucas looked out the window, his mind racing with questions about the impact he truly wanted to make.

His attention drifted toward his laptop where he began to search for answers. After an hour or two, Lucas's eyes were weary from scrolling through online forums, coaching methodologies, and articles on transformative practices. His search was aimless at first, a mix of keywords that reflected his inner turmoil: "deep transformation coaching," "beyond action plans in coaching," "coaching for sustainable change."

It was during this digital expedition that he stumbled upon a blog post titled "The Art of Transformation: Going Beyond the Surface in Coaching." The article was an interview with Marina Cooper, a name Lucas wasn't familiar with, but by the end of the first paragraph, he was captivated.

Marina spoke of her journey from a high-powered lawyer to a coach and mentor focused on the depths of human potential. As Lucas absorbed Marina's words, he found himself drawn into the narrative of her transformation.

She described her pivotal moment, a realization that the essence of true transformation in coaching extended far beyond tangible skill sets and strategic action plans. It was rooted, she revealed, in a deep exploration of one's being—a path she had courageously embarked upon herself before attempting to guide others.

Her story was a beacon for Lucas, illuminating the uncharted territories of human potential he had imagined but hadn't known how to explore. Marina's transition was not just a change in career but a metamorphosis in understanding of what it meant to evoke change in others.

Then the narrative unfolded further, introducing a concept that captivated Lucas's imagination. Marina detailed the creation of a retreat, a labor of love that she established on a remote island. This place, she explained, was a manifestation of her coaching ethos, designed as a sanctuary for those coaches and leaders brave enough to explore the depths of their capabilities and passion for change.

The retreat, set against a backdrop of natural beauty, offered an immersion into an environment where silence spoke as loudly as words, where nature's rhythms invited introspection, and where each experience was an invitation to look inward. It was a space dedicated to uncovering and harnessing the power within, through a blend of solitude, communal sharing, and guided discovery.

What captured Lucas's attention most wasn't just the idyllic description of the retreat but the intention behind it. The retreat embodied a belief in the potential of connecting deeply with oneself, with others, and with the natural world. It promised an exploration that went beyond the conventional bounds of coaching into the realm of personal evolution.

In the quiet of his office, the yearning for depth in his coaching practice found its echo in her words, offering a glimpse of the path he sought. It was as if Marina had charted a course through the very questions that plagued him, and the retreat was the compass pointing toward the answers.

Lucas navigated through the website, each click deepening his resolve. Here, in the digital footprint of Marina's retreat, he saw the opportunity to elevate his approach to coaching and his ability to deeply connect with himself and others.

The final push came from a passage on the site: "Transformation begins when we dare to step beyond the familiar shores of our knowledge."

With a clarity that surprised him, Lucas knew he had to reach out. He found the page where an invitation to inquire about the retreat awaited. Typing with a sense of purpose he hadn't felt in months, Lucas crafted a message to Marina, introducing himself and expressing his desire to learn the deeper level of coaching she spoke of. His heart raced as he hit "send," marking the beginning of a journey he hoped would redefine his career.

Lucas took a moment to absorb the magnitude of his decision. He had crossed an invisible threshold, stepping into a future charged with the promise of discovery and growth. With the night deepening around him, Lucas felt a deep sense of peace. For the first time in a long while, he was truly ready to embrace the unknown. Ahead lay a path to redefine his coaching practice and rediscover himself in ways he had yet to imagine.

Setting Sail to Discovery

Traveling to the island felt like crossing into another world. After a long plane ride, Lucas boarded the small boat that would take him to the retreat location. The mainland faded into the distance, and with it, the persona of Lucas the coach, the consultant, the strategist. What remained was simply Lucas, a seeker on the precipice of discovery.

The boat cut through the waves, a solitary vessel against the vast expanse of the sea. The rhythm of the water against the hull became a meditative backdrop to Lucas's thoughts. He had left behind the familiar to seek out the essence of transformation, and the weight of that decision settled around him like a cloak.

As the island came into view, Lucas felt a stir of anticipation. The retreat was nestled on a stunning island, a place untouched by the rush of modern life. The natural beauty of the island was breathtaking—a lush landscape that promised solitude and the space to explore the depths of one's being.

Lucas's first steps onto the island were met with an unexpected yet refreshing greeting. Marina stood there, embodying an air of approachability. "Ah, Lucas! Welcome to the edge of the known world," she said, her voice rich with excitement. "I hope you didn't bring a suitcase full of answers. We tend to travel light here."

Her authenticity intrigued Lucas. He chuckled, "I left most of my luggage behind, but I think I've got a few hidden answers tucked away."

"Perfect," Marina responded. "We'll have you unpack those in no time. Answers tend to weigh us down more than we realize."

As they walked, Lucas was struck by the serene beauty of the island, but it was Marina's candidness that caught his attention. He seized the opportunity to learn more about her.

"So, from courtrooms to island sanctuaries, that's quite the leap. What sparked that shift?"

Marina chuckled, "Ah, the age-old quest for meaning," she began. "I was knee-deep in legal briefs when I realized I was more passionate about arguing over dinner menus than court cases."

Lucas laughed, drawn in by her honesty. "And that led you here?"

"In a manner of speaking," Marina responded, her gaze drifting to the canopy above. "I took what I thought would be a brief sabbatical. Wanted to clear my head and find some peace."

"And instead, you found...?"

"Isaac," she said, her voice softening at the name.

"It was so curious, really," Marina began, her voice taking on a reflective tone. "I was here for just a few days when I heard about a hidden waterfall on the island, a place of supposed unparalleled beauty. My attempt to find it, however, turned into an exercise in getting hopelessly lost."

She described wandering through parts of the island not marked on any map, driven by a deep yearning for something she couldn't quite articulate. "And then, there it was—not the waterfall, but a quaint, almost mystical cabin, ensconced in an untouched part of the island. Isaac was sitting outside, as if he'd been waiting for me."

"What was your first impression of him?" he asked.

"I thought he was a figment of my imagination," Marina admitted with a laugh. "He had this timeless quality about him, like a character from a storybook. His hair and beard were white as the frothy waves, and his eyes... sky blue, they held a kind of wisdom and peace I'd never seen in anyone."

Marina recounted her initial skepticism, how her trained, analytical mind struggled to take Isaac seriously. "He spoke of listening to the silence, of understanding the language of the heart, and other concepts that my lawyer-brain dismissed as 'nutty'."

"But you kept going back to him," Lucas noted, intrigued by the shift in Marina's demeanor as she spoke of Isaac.

"Every evening for ten days," she confirmed. "With each visit, my skepticism was replaced by a genuine curiosity. Isaac had a way of simplifying the complex, of making the intangible seem tangible. And he never directly answered my questions; instead, he guided me to find the answers within myself."

"What was the turning point for you?" Lucas asked.

Marina paused; her gaze distant as she recalled the moment. "One evening, under a sky full of stars, Isaac said to me, 'Being lost is just an opportunity to find a path you never knew you were looking for.' It was then I realized I wasn't just lost in the woods that day; I was lost in life. Isaac helped me find my path."

"And now you're helping others find theirs," Lucas observed.

Marina smiled, a genuine expression of contentment spreading across her face. "That's the hope. Isaac's teachings gave me a new perspective. I wanted to share that, to create a space where others could explore their own depths."

Their conversation continued as they meandered through the retreat site, with Marina sharing more about her vision.

As they concluded their walk, Lucas felt a surge of gratitude for having met Marina and an eagerness to dive into the exciting week that awaited him. Marina, with her wisdom and warmth, had piqued his curiosity and offered him a glimpse into the upcoming journey of self-discovery.

Unveiling the Path Ahead

After Lucas settled into his accommodation—a yurt that struck the perfect balance between simplicity and subtle luxury— Marina appeared at the door, "I hope you find your accommodation comfortable," she said. "Remember, dinner at the beachside restaurant at 7 pm sharp. It's a casual affair, but it marks the beginning of our time together." Lucas nodded, still absorbing the serene beauty of his surroundings.

As he made his way to the restaurant later that evening, the path illuminated by tiki torches, he felt a mix of anticipation and nervousness.

The setting for dinner was straight out of a dream. The restaurant, open-air and illuminated by strung lanterns and candles, exuded a warmth that eased some of Lucas's nerves. He spotted Marina instantly, her bright orange dress a beacon in the dim evening light, gathered at a large round table with four other retreat participants. Lucas, taking a deep breath, approached and introduced himself, his voice steadier than he felt inside.

Pangs of self-doubt crept in as he took the last seat at the table, silently questioning his place among these strangers. Marina, ever the perceptive host, sensed Lucas's discomfort and quickly diffused it with a light-hearted joke that broke the ice for the entire group.

As introductions went around, Lucas's initial feelings of doubt began to fade. One participant, a seasoned executive, shared her reasons for coming to the retreat—seeking clarity and direction in a world that valued noise over silence. Another, a successful entrepreneur, spoke of her desire to lead with empathy rather than authority, to inspire rather than command. The remaining two participants were coaches who, like Lucas, were looking for ways to deepen their impact with clients.

Marina's natural grace facilitated the conversations, ensuring everyone felt seen and heard. She then took a moment to address the group. "Over the next week," she began, "you'll embark on a journey unlike any other. This isn't just about acquiring skills or strategies; it's about evolving from the inside out."

With the backdrop of the softly lit beach, she detailed all that lay ahead. "Each morning, you will be presented with a challenge that will support you in elevating your personal impact" she began, her voice carrying the wisdom gleaned from her time with Isaac. "These challenges are gateways to embodying the essence of mastery that goes beyond professional roles and resonates with the very core of who you are."

She then revealed a captivating element of their island retreat, one that instantly sparked Lucas's curiosity. "Each day," Marina continued, "offers you a canvas as vast as the island itself. After our morning meeting, you'll have the opportunity to explore, to wander, to reflect, and—most importantly—to engage with these beautiful surroundings."

Marina explained that part of their work involved being open to random interactions with the island and its inhabitants. "Stay alert to the opportunities that present themselves. The embodiment of the day's challenge may come through in the most unexpected ways, as you offer your curiosity, your listening, and your presence to the island."

Lucas found the concept exhilarating. "It's in these interactions," Marina emphasized, "that you'll be faced with the opportunity to meet the challenge, do something different, and learn powerful practices that enrich both giver and receiver."

The retreat, as outlined by Marina, was an invitation to engage fully, stay present with his surroundings, and remain open to growth opportunities, both professional and personal.

That night, Lucas lay in his yurt. He closed his eyes, took a deep breath, and with hopeful anticipation drifted into a peaceful sleep, eager to awaken to the first day of what promised to be a life-changing experience.

DAY 1

Harvesting Belief

AS THE NEW DAY DAWNED, THE WEATHER reflected the anticipation Lucas felt: the sky was overcast, with the sun starting to peek through the clouds. Despite the serene surroundings, a nervous energy buzzed in Lucas's belly as he made his way to the communal table for breakfast. The air was charged with expectation, not just from Lucas, but from all the participants, each one curious about the day's offerings.

Marina greeted everyone with her characteristic warmth. As they settled down, the aroma of fresh coffee and pastries filled the air, creating a comforting backdrop to the gathering.

"Good morning, everyone," Marina began. "Today, we embark on a journey that goes to the very heart of what it means to coach and lead others."

Marina's conviction was palpable, her passion shining through each word she spoke.

"Your first challenge will offer you the opportunity to see the value in having faith in the abilities, creativity, and potential of those you support, be they clients, employees, or team members. It's about empowering them to tap into their own well of knowledge and strength."

The group nodded, the importance of this concept beginning to resonate with them. Marina paused for a moment, allowing her words to sink in before she added, "Remember, people are the experts in their own life, work, family, feelings, and values. Our role is not to overshadow them with *our* knowledge or ideas but to foster a space where *theirs* can emerge. Therefore, we start with your first, and may I say most foundational challenge: Believe in others *more* than yourself. In other words, trust that people have everything they need and that they are whole and resourceful enough to find their own answers. They just need your help to access them."

As Lucas absorbed Marina's words, he found the concept challenging. The idea of stepping back, of placing more faith in the client than in his own expertise, was a shift from his usual approach.

Marina invoked a poignant lesson from Isaac to highlight the essence of the day's challenge. "Isaac would often emphasize how our belief in others could ignite their self-belief," she reflected, her voice imbued with a touch of nostalgia. "And from my own journey, I can affirm the truth in his words. Isaac had this unwavering belief in me, even at times when my own faith in myself wavered. It was his steadfast confidence that nurtured and eventually helped me cultivate my own." Her acknowledgment served as a testament to Isaac's wisdom and as a living example of the transformative power of belief.

"So, as you go about your day, I invite you each to deeply reflect on this foundational tenet and look for opportunities to genuinely practice believing in those you interact with, whether they're fellow participants or members of the island community. Pay close attention to how this belief subtly influences the dynamics of your conversations with others, the decisions they make, and their own confidence in themselves."

She paused, allowing her words to land with each person seated around the table. "Consider how believing in others more than yourself can alter your approach to coaching and leadership and the very essence of how people feel supported."

Marina's eyes swept across the group. "Notice the shifts, however small, that occur when you lead with faith in another's potential. Watch how confidence blooms in spaces where individuals feel deeply seen and believed in. And equally, be mindful of moments where doubt might cloud that belief and reflect on the effect it has."

She encouraged them to approach the day as an experiment in weaving this idea into the fabric of their interactions. "This is about redefining how you engage with others. Every conversation, every encounter today is an opportunity to embody this principle and observe the ripple effects it creates."

The breakfast gathering disbanded, each participant stepping into the day armed with a new lens through which to view their interactions and the transformative potential they held.

Lucas found a secluded spot near the shoreline that provided a tranquil backdrop for reflection. He sat, gazing out at the horizon. Marina's challenge to believe in others more than yourself created a feeling of resistance within him.

He acknowledged the discomfort, turning it over in his mind. Lucas had always prided himself on his expertise, his ability to guide clients through complex situations with the wisdom he had accumulated over the years. The idea of placing more faith in his clients' abilities than in his own expertise felt counterintuitive.

As a seasoned professional, Lucas understood the value of his knowledge. It had been his compass, guiding his clients away from pitfalls and towards success. The thought nagged at him: how could valuing his clients' insights more than his own be the right approach? Wouldn't his experience help them avoid mistakes, fast-track their learning, and navigate their paths more effectively?

Lucas began to question what his resistance might be rooted in. Could it be the fear of relinquishing control or not bringing value to his clients? This concept clearly challenged the traditional dynamics he was accustomed to.

With a mind swirling with thoughts, Lucas stood up, brushed the sand off his pants, and embarked on a hike through the island's lush landscape. The dense canopy above filtered the sunlight, and the air was filled with the rich scents of foliage. This environment, so different from his usual surroundings, seemed to invite deeper reflection, a chance to ponder Marina's first challenge away from the distraction of his normal life.

As he wandered, lost in thought, Lucas stumbled upon a community garden nestled in a clearing. Three islanders stood among rows of vibrant greenery; their expressions marked by concern as they discussed a pressing issue. The main crop, a staple in the islanders' diet, was afflicted with a disease that threatened its survival.

Lucas paused, overhearing their conversation. His initial instinct was to offer assistance by drawing upon the knowledge he had acquired from a gardening hobby back home. With a desire to help, he approached the group and shared his proposed solution, confident that his external perspective could save the crop.

The islanders listened politely to Lucas's suggestion before responding with skepticism. Their gentle rebuttals revealed an understanding of their crops that Lucas hadn't considered.

But fueled by a desire to prove his worth, Lucas pressed on, attempting to convince them that his solution might work. However, it quickly became apparent that his ideas were not at all resonating with his audience.

As Lucas stood among the doubtful islanders, feeling the weight of his misjudgment, one of them moved in closely toward him. She was a woman whose face bore the soft lines of years and the deep knowledge that came from a lifetime of living on the island. Her eyes met Lucas's as she began to speak.

"Lucas, our island is much like a delicate tapestry," she started. "Each thread represents a different part of our ecosystem, woven together over generations."

She stooped down, her fingers brushing against the leaves of a plant. "See here," she continued, pointing to a barely noticeable insect on the underside of the leaf. "This little one is part of why our crops thrive. The balance here is delicate. Introducing something new or foreign, as you suggested, could lead to unraveling."

Lucas listened, humbled by her knowledge. The woman went on to describe how the islanders had learned to observe the signs of their environment—the way certain birds' arrival signaled the best time to plant, how the direction of the wind could predict the health of the crops, and how the color of the ocean could indicate changes in the weather that would affect their harvest.

"Your solution, though well-intentioned, doesn't take into account these signs, Lucas, and eventually it could cause more harm than good."

Her words were not a reprimand but a lesson, a reminder of the importance of humility, of recognizing the limits of one's own knowledge.

Lucas felt a great respect for the elder and the wisdom she embodied. Her explanation of the island's ecology, a system so finely tuned that even the smallest change could have unforeseen consequences, was a revelation. It was an illustration of the first challenge in a context far removed from coaching yet deeply relevant to his process of understanding.

Lucas stood within the garden, a realization washing over him. In his eagerness to help, he had placed too much faith in his own knowledge, overlooking the invaluable experience of the islanders. He had, in essence, failed the first challenge Marina had proposed that morning: to believe in others—even more than himself.

This was a humbling lesson in the importance of true partnership. Lucas had sought to be a solver of problems but learned instead that the role of a true helper was to uplift the wisdom of those he aimed to help.

As he said goodbye to the elder and departed, Lucas felt a visceral shift within himself. The resistance that had clouded his morning had given way to a newfound respect for the knowledge present in the community. This encounter had provided him with a precious insight that he would carry with him for the remainder of the retreat and the rest of his coaching career.

As he headed back toward town he continued to process this revelation. He thought to himself: "The challenge isn't asking me to devalue my knowledge but to recognize that the essence of true support comes from helping others tap into their own strengths, knowledge, and creativity. It's a partnership, not a hierarchy—and it requires a shift in perspective, from being the sage on the stage to being a guide on the side."

Thrilled with both his poetic skills and this enlightening revelation, Lucas smiled to himself and wondered out loud, "How could this have eluded me all these years?"

Back at the retreat site, the day gave way to the soft hues of evening. After dinner, sitting around the bonfire, Lucas found himself deep in conversation with a fellow retreat participant, Elizabeth, a corporate leader from London whose sharp acumen had led her company through tumultuous times. Their conversation, initially revolving around the day's challenge, gradually deepened into an exchange of insights and experiences.

Elizabeth, with a thoughtful pause, initiated the reflection. "Lucas, what occurred in the garden today is a vivid reminder of a truth we often overlook. In our roles as leaders and coaches, it's not about having all the answers, but about embracing the vulnerability of not knowing, of being learners ourselves."

Lucas, absorbing her words, felt a resonance within. "Yes, it was a humbling realization. I went in there thinking I could be the hero with a solution. Instead, I learned that real support lies in fostering an environment where answers can surface from the collective wisdom present."

"The real lesson," Elizabeth continued, "is in recognizing the power of curiosity and approaching each interaction as a partner in discovery."

Lucas nodded, "It's a shift from imposing our views to facilitating a space where the best solutions can emerge. It demands humility to admit that, despite our experience, we don't have all the answers."

Their conversation began exploring how this lesson could be applied to the broader spectrum of coaching and leadership. "It's about changing our stance," Lucas mused, "from teaching and telling to listening and learning, from directing to empowering."

As they concluded their exchange, both Lucas and Elizabeth acknowledged the deep impact of this lesson. They recognized that their growth lay not in relying on the knowledge and resources they had, but in valuing the wisdom of those they supported.

"This challenge," Lucas said as they parted ways for the night, "has reshaped my understanding of what it means to be truly helpful. It's about of becoming more inquisitive, more humble, and ultimately, more effective in empowering others."

Shortly after Lucas walked away from his conversation with Elizabeth, he began to feel turmoil brewing inside him. Each step back to his yurt was heavy with a newfound realization that left him feeling startled, remorseful, and even a tad embarrassed. His mind replayed countless coaching sessions where he had eagerly dispensed his business acumen, tools, and best practices, believing he was guiding his clients toward solutions. "Was that approach erroneous?" he pondered. The pride he once felt in his ability to help his clients now seemed to cast a long shadow of doubt. "Have I been more of a crutch than a catalyst?" he questioned silently.

In a moment of urgent need for clarity, Lucas turned on his heel and sought out Marina. He found her by the bonfire as she gathered her belongings. Lucas approached hesitantly, sharing his revelation, confusion, and the whirlwind of emotions that the challenge had stirred within him.

Marina listened with attentiveness, her eyes reflecting a depth of understanding. "Lucas," she began, "there's no wrongdoing in the way you've supported others. Each journey is unique, and the methods you've employed have brought value to your clients. That's evident." Her words, spoken with such genuine reassurance, began to soothe Lucas's thoughts. "But you're here because you believe there's another level, a way to elevate your impact. Isn't that why you came?"

As Marina's words washed over him, Lucas felt a shift within. "So, you're saying there's value in both approaches?" he asked.

"Yes, Lucas," Marina responded with a gentle nod. "Every method has its place. It's like having different tools in your toolbox. The key is knowing when to use each one."

Lucas let out a slow breath. "I guess I've been so focused on being the one with the answers that I forgot to consider the value of my clients' wisdom and experience," he admitted.

"This is very common, Lucas. Recognizing it is the first step towards growth. This new approach is about partnership, about walking alongside someone in their discovery, not leading them."

He nodded, a sense of peace beginning to seep in. "Walking alongside," he repeated, the words resonating with a newfound understanding of his role as a fellow traveler on the path of discovery.

"Yes," he acknowledged, his voice steadier, "I see now that this new approach, focusing on empowering rather than instructing, feels easier and scalable." The idea was crystallizing within him. "It opens up the possibility of helping *anyone* on *any* topic, not only within my areas of expertise."

Marina's smile was encouraging. "Exactly, Lucas. What you're learning here, to believe in others more than yourself, can bring about profound revelations to *anyone* dealing with *any* issue."

As she stood to leave, Marina's parting words were tinged with a bit of wit. "Besides, think of all the extra energy you'll have now that you're not trying to solve everyone's problems."

Lucas couldn't help but laugh, the tension easing from his shoulders. The challenge had opened his eyes to a new way of being, and he liked it.

The night closed in around Lucas, but the darkness felt lighter, filled with promise. As he retraced his steps back to his yurt, he felt renewed and eager to explore the depths of coaching through this new lens.

DAY 2

Unearthing Gems

THE NEXT DAY, UNDER THE WARM GLOW OF THE morning sun, the retreat participants gathered for breakfast. Marina, with her usual warmth, welcomed everyone before posing a question: Who felt they succeeded with yesterday's challenge, and would they be willing to share?

After a few moments of hesitation, Brandon, a twenty-something with an unmistakably hipster vibe, slowly raised his hand. His distinctive style—a combination of vintage and modern—made him stand out, but it was his earnest expression that caught everyone's attention.

"Well, so I had this really enlightening experience yesterday," Brandon began, tucking a lock of hair behind his ear. "I was walking in town when I met Lena, this cool local artist. She's working on a huge mural about the island's history, and she told me that she felt stuck, kinda like writer's block, but for artists, right? And so, I'm thinking I'm gonna swoop in and save the day by helping her get out of this slump. You know, I was all ready to share my brilliant ideas."

He air-quoted the word 'brilliant,' drawing a ripple of laughter around the table. "But then, I just forced myself to zip it and instead I thought it would be better if I just asked her some questions. So, I thought for a minute and then asked her, "What about the island's history really speaks to you?"

"Wow, that's a great coaching question, Brandon." Marina said through a smile.

"Thanks! And then later I asked her what kind of ideas came to mind when she thought about this."

"And what did you notice in Lena when you approached the conversation that way?" Marina prodded.

"It was epic! Like watching someone light up from the inside," Brandon said. "Lena, she just... she knew so much more than I could've imagined. And when I actually listened, it was clear any idea I had wouldn't have compared to what she came up with."

Marina nodded, encouraging him to continue. "Was there a noticeable difference in how she saw her own abilities?"

"Absolutely," Brandon confirmed. "I mean, it was like I could see her believing in herself more and more with each question I asked. Her confidence just soared. It was awesome."

He leaned back, reflecting on the transformation he witnessed. "Believing in her more than I believed in my own ideas made me feel smart in a way. More than that, it felt right. I realized that my value wasn't in giving her *my* ideas, but in tapping *her* creativity and passion."

Marina smiled. "So, Brandon, which approach do you prefer now?" she asked, already knowing the answer.

Brandon's response was infused with enthusiasm. "Oh, this new approach, absolutely. It opens up a whole new dimension of interactions, you know? Instead of just dishing out advice based on what I know, it's about unlocking others' potential. It feels more genuine, and... honestly, a lot easier. Cuz let's be real, it's incredibly freeing to not have to know the answer but instead help someone else find their answer. That's the magic." Marina's expression reflected her pride in Brandon's understanding. "Well said, Brandon. Well said."

Lucas couldn't help but feel a kinship with the young man. It reinforced the power of genuinely believing in others, a lesson he was beginning to internalize, but realized it may take some practice to fully get there.

◆

Marina, with the group's full attention, capitalized on Brandon's insightful story as the perfect segue into the day's challenge. "Brandon's experience beautifully sets the stage for what comes next. As coaches and leaders, our toolboxes are rich with questions, yet the art lies in choosing the right ones to ask," she began.

"We've all been trained to navigate towards solutions, to ask about actions, plans, and goals. It's a strategy designed to tackle problems head-on, to extinguish fires, and chart paths forward. We might ask questions like, 'What can you do?', 'What needs to change?', 'How can you adapt?', or 'Who can you ask for help?' And while these are undoubtedly valuable, there exists another realm of questioning, one less employed but incredibly effective."

Marina glanced at each participant, her eyes settling on the ocean visible from the dining area. "So, I'd like you all to finish your breakfast and meet me at the beach," she announced. "There, you will experience firsthand what I'm talking about. Come ready to get dirty and dig deep—both metaphorically and literally." Her words sparking curiosity among the group as they anticipated the upcoming activity.

<hr />

Thirty minutes later, the retreat participants gathered on the soft, white sands of the beach. They formed a loose circle around Marina, the atmosphere ripe with curiosity.

"Today," Marina began, "we're going to explore what lies beneath the surface. Much like the sand under our feet hides shells and sea glass, the people you work with often have deeper truths waiting to be acknowledged and understood."

She handed each person a small trowel. "This is your tool to unearth objects in the sand, but it also represents your role in revealing the deeper aspects of someone's being." Marina continued, "I want you to find a spot on the beach and observe what lies *on* the surface. After taking a good look, begin to dig. Dig until you find something that lies *beneath* the surface."

The group spread out along the beach, each one claiming their section and observing the contents readily visible on the sand before beginning to dig. Marina walked amongst them, observing their progress. "As you search, consider how this is like coaching. We see the surface, the presented issue, but often, it's not what's immediately visible that holds the key to transformation."

As the participants dug deeper, Marina called out, "Think of each dig as an inquiry into the person's world. It's not just about their actions and words—but what's buried deep within. Their fears, their dreams, their beliefs, and their values."

After a while, Marina called everyone back to the circle to share their findings—a colorful mix of shells, smooth stones, coins, and even an old, rusted piece of metal. Each item, once concealed beneath the sand, now had a story to tell.

Marina picked up a piece of beautiful green sea glass. "Consider this piece of glass," she suggested. "It's been shaped and buffed by the water and sand over time, much like our lives have shaped us. It might not look significant at first, but it has a story, a history that adds to its character."

"Now," Marina said, holding up a particularly unique shell, "think of this shell as an aspect of someone's inner world. It was there all along, but it required patience and a willingness to dig deep to bring it to light. Your questions, like these trowels, are the tools that help uncover the valuable parts of others that are not on display."

She continued, "Just as you unearthed these hidden items, we aim to uncover the less visible aspects of people's lives. It's about going deeper, beyond the obvious, to help them explore their internal landscape."

"Let's reflect. How did it feel to search for something without knowing what you would find?"

Lucas was the first to respond. "It was odd at first, not knowing what I was looking for. But then, it became exciting, like every scoop of sand might reveal something new." He paused, considering the deeper implication. "It's kind of like when we first start with a client. We don't really know what's under the surface, but as we dig deeper, we discover things that even they might not be aware of."

Brandon nodded in agreement, adding, "Yeah, I guess we have to be okay with not knowing. We just give the space and support for people to find their own truths, without predicting what those truths might be."

Marina smiled, pleased with their insights. "Exactly," she affirmed. "It's about curiosity. By being curious about their inner worlds, we allow others to explore and reveal new awareness. Digging in the sand today didn't guarantee what we would find, but it was the act of searching that was important."

The group nodded, their expressions reflective as they absorbed the lesson, connecting the beach activity to their roles as coaches and leaders.

Marina continued, "We're facilitating a deeper exploration of the self. In doing so, we can help others find their own unique solutions that are as real as these artifacts you've unearthed today. Beneath the surface of every challenge, like the sands of this beach, lie little gems for self-discovery."

Marina paused, making sure her words resonated deeply with the group.

"As I mentioned this morning," she continued, "you are all adept at navigating towards solutions, at asking what actions can be taken to solve problems or what resources one can tap into. This approach is undoubtedly valuable, but if we want to help affect lasting change in people's lives, we need to dig deeper, to unearth the obstacles and knowledge within them."

She took a step closer to the group, her expression earnest. "Instead of focusing solely on what a person can *do*, we turn our attention inward, asking about who they *are*. It's about their being—how they feel, what they value, what they believe, and what they fear. This shift from doing to being," Marina gestured towards the sand around them, "opens up a space for awareness, for insights that might otherwise remain buried. By asking these deeper, more personal questions, we help people understand themselves better, and also understand what might be standing in their way."

She continued, drawing upon Isaac's wisdom, "Isaac would often say that reaching one's true potential starts with uncovering the internal obstacles—those limiting beliefs, stories, and fears that hold us back. He believed that what's happening on the inside inevitably shapes our external realities."

With a thoughtful look, Marina laid out the day's challenge, "So, your challenge today is to inquire more about the BEING than the DOING. Be genuinely curious about people's inner world—their feelings, dreams, strengths, fears—rather than just the possible actions they can take or plans they can make. This approach fosters deeper understanding and connection, while empowering them to discover solutions that resonate with who they are."

Lucas raised his hand, a slight furrow forming between his brows. "So, we're not supposed to ask about what they can do to solve their problem, but instead, we should ask them questions about themselves?" he asked, trying to grasp the concept.

Marina responded warmly, "Exactly, Lucas. The idea is to first focus on their internal world, before helping them to devise an action plan. If we only focus on what they can do to fix a problem without identifying the story or belief behind it, it's merely a temporary fix—a band aid. To foster sustainable change, we need to encourage them to look inward first."

Lucas nodded, his expression clearing as he understood. "So, it's like shining a light on the actual problem that lies inside before addressing the external problem," he reflected aloud.

"That's precisely it," Marina confirmed with a nod. "But not only problems, but skills, values, and beliefs too. That's how masterful coaches operate. They help people understand themselves better so that any action plan they develop is informed by a deep understanding of their own barriers and strengths."

Marina's challenge sparked a curious energy among the participants. The notion of shifting focus from the external to the internal, from action to essence, promised a day of rich exploration and learning.

Lucas ventured out with a sense of excitement. The challenge for today aligned with what he believed was the missing piece in elevating his coaching. The idea of probing deeper into the "being" rather than the "doing" of his clients intrigued him, yet he couldn't shake off a twinge of apprehension. How would his clients react to this shift in approach? Known for his ability to drive results and action, Lucas pondered the potential resistance he might face for delving into more personal, existential inquiries.

With these thoughts swirling in his mind, Lucas decided to mull over the day's challenge in a more casual setting. He soon found himself at "The Island Brew," a quaint coffee shop whose name carried the charm of its surroundings. After ordering a latte, he spotted an open seat at one of the communal tables. He was soon joined by a young man with a vibrant energy that seemed to contradict the tranquil pace of island life.

The young man extended a friendly hand. "Hey, I'm Kai," he introduced himself with a welcoming smile.

Lucas returned the gesture, feeling the warmth of Kai's greeting. "Lucas. Nice to meet you, Kai. What brings you to this spot today?"

As Kai took a notebook out of his bag, his eyes sparkled with hope. "I'm just here trying to catch some inspiration," he shared. "I've got all these big ideas, trying to figure out how to bring them to life on the mainland. I want to make a big impact there." He paused, his expression reflecting a bit of restlessness. "Have you ever felt like you're meant to do something more?"

Lucas couldn't help but smile. "Wow, you have no idea," he responded.

Lucas settled into the conversation, intrigued by Kai's restless energy. "Kai, I'm curious," Lucas began. "You mentioned wanting to make a big impact on the mainland. Can I ask you some questions to explore that a bit more? I'm practicing a new coaching approach."

Kai, his curiosity piqued by Lucas's proposal, nodded. "Yeah, sure. That sounds interesting."

Lucas leaned in, his coach's intuition guiding him. "What is it about leaving the island that feels necessary for you to make this impact?"

Kai's response was quick, "It's like the island is too small for what I envision. I want to do big things, you know? Things I can't do here."

Lucas, remembering Marina's challenge, gently shifted the focus. "I understand wanting to do big things. But let's try something different for a moment. Beyond what you can *do*, who do you want to *be* in the process?

Kai paused, the shift in questioning prompting him to reflect deeper. After what felt like a whole minute, Kai replied, "I guess...I want to be someone who inspires, who creates change through creativity. Someone who's a leader but in a way that brings people together."

Encouraged by Kai's openness, Lucas took a breath and pressed further. "Those are strong qualities. How are those aspects of who you want to be already present in your life here on the island?"

Kai considered Lucas's question. "I suppose I'm already on that path in small ways here. For example, I organize beach cleanups and help out at the community center."

"Hmmm," Lucas said. "It sounds like you're already embodying those qualities you admire. What's missing for you then?"

"I'm not sure. It just feels like it has to be bigger, ya know?" replied Kai.

"I hear you," Lucas replied. "What are some bigger opportunities that you haven't seized yet?"

"Well, I had this crazy idea of running for mayor of this town. But that seems like a pipe dream."

"What makes you call it a 'crazy idea' and a 'pipe dream'?" Lucas asked thoughtfully.

Kai shifted uncomfortably, the question uncovering thoughts he hadn't fully acknowledged before. "I guess," he started, hesitating, "it's because I'm afraid. Um, afraid of failing, especially here, in my own town. ...If I fail elsewhere, it's one thing, but here, it feels like there's more at stake."

Lucas nodded, understanding the weight of Kai's admission. "Fear of failure is incredibly common, especially when it comes to the people and places we care about most. Are you willing to explore that fear a bit?"

"Sure," replied Kai.

Lucas asked, "What makes failing here at home feel particularly daunting to you?"

Kai took a deep breath. "Failing here means letting down the very community that raised me. It's like...I know everyone and everything here, failing here would feel unbearable?"

"I totally get that," Lucas's voice soft but firm. "What would it mean to *succeed* here, where you have roots and a genuine understanding of the community's needs?"

Kai was silent for a moment. "It would be amazing. But I never thought about that possibility because I've been so focused on the idea of leaving. Hmm...maybe...I don't know...maybe I've overlooked the potential right in front of me."

Lucas leaned in. "Your idea of running for mayor doesn't sound like a pipe dream to me. It sounds like a deep-seated desire to contribute, to use your creativity in a leadership role that could truly benefit your community."

Kai's eyes lit up with a mixture of realization and determination. "Wow. I've been running from the fear of failure when I could be channeling that energy into making a real difference here."

Lucas smiled as he witnessed Kai coming to terms with his fears and recognizing his potential.

As their conversation unfolded, Lucas was mindful to keep his inquiries focused on Kai's being—his values, strengths, and desires. Each question was an invitation for Kai to dive deeper into his own self-awareness, and away from the need to find a geographical solution to his yearning for impact.

By the end of their conversation, Kai felt a shift within himself. The fear of failure was still there, but it no longer held the same paralyzing grip. Through Lucas's coaching, he began to see his fear as a signpost, pointing him towards the areas where he had the most to offer and where the stakes felt highest because they mattered most.

Leaving the coffee shop, both men carried with them a new awareness. For Kai, it was the realization that his dreams of making a significant impact could start right here on the island, and that confronting his fear of failure was the first step toward that goal. For Lucas, the conversation was a testament to the power of converting fear into action, further deepening his commitment to exploring the 'being' over the 'doing' in his coaching practice.

◆

Lucas made his way back to the retreat for lunch, his interaction with Kai echoing in his mind. The day's challenge had revealed itself to be an impactful learning opportunity that he was eager to share with Marina.

Finding Marina in the lounge, Lucas approached her. "Marina, do you have a moment? I'd like to share something about the challenge today," he asked.

Marina, always ready to listen and learn, nodded. "Of course, Lucas. I'd love to hear about it."

Lucas recounted his conversation with Kai, detailing how he shifted the focus from doing to being, and how it opened a pathway for Kai to see his potential and fears in a new light. Marina listened intently, her eyes reflecting the pride she felt in Lucas's application of the day's lesson.

When Lucas finished, Marina congratulated him. "That's wonderful, Lucas. You've embodied today's challenge beautifully. How do you feel about this new approach now that you've experienced it firsthand?"

Lucas replied, "I feel good about it, especially because Kai was so receptive. But I can't help worrying about my current clients back home. They're used to me helping them tackle problems directly, focusing on actions and solutions. I'm not sure how they'll respond to a deeper exploration of their inner world."

"Lucas, let me share a story Isaac once told me." Marina began. "On this very island there once was a gardener who grew the most exquisite flowers. These flowers had the power to bring joy to anyone who smelled them. Eager to share this joy, the gardener would invite the forest creatures to his garden."

"But, you see, not all creatures were drawn to the flowers. The deer loved them, and the butterflies too, but the bees were too busy, and the night creatures slept through the day. The gardener quickly learned that he could not compel the creatures to come. He could only tend to his garden, keeping the flowers vibrant and fragrant, hoping that those who wanted joy would find their way."

"Like the gardener, you have found something precious that can help others. Yet, like the creatures of the forest, some may not be ready to accept it or interested in receiving it. All creatures have their paths to follow and the most you can do is provide opportunities for support. Those who are ready or interested will accept it."

Lucas pondered the essence of the story—we can offer the opportunity for deeper exploration, but we can't force anyone to accept it.

Marina continued, her tone encouraging. "The beauty of coaching lies in offering these opportunities for growth and being there to support those who are ready and willing. Whether your clients back home will be open to this style of inquiry is uncertain, but it's essential to offer it. Like with Kai, you never know who might be on the cusp of a significant breakthrough. The important thing is that when a client is ready for deeper exploration, you'll be there to support them. If they're not ready, your best bet is to just meet them where they are."

Lucas absorbed Marina's words, the analogy settling the turmoil within him. The notion that not everyone would be ready for such an approach but that it was still worth offering was a comforting resolution to his concerns.

The encounter with Kai, bolstered by Marina's wisdom, reinforced his commitment to offer deeper inquiry to those willing to embark on the journey.

As the sun began its slow descent, Lucas found a quiet spot on the beach to reflect on his day. It was here, in this serene setting, that he realized the retreat was offering him much more than he had anticipated. He understood now that coaching was an art form, one that required a diverse palette of approaches to meet the unique needs of each client.

Marina's words echoed in his mind, a reminder that these new techniques were to be used indiscriminately, when the moment was right.

The revelation that not every client would be receptive to every method, or even require them, was initially surprising. Yet, as he sat there, watching the day give way to night, Lucas embraced this understanding with an open heart. He recognized the value of having a versatile coaching toolbox, equipped with strategies for action but also with approaches that focused on the person's being. This duality, he realized, was the essence of masterful coaching.

As he stood up, leaving the tranquility of the beach behind, Lucas felt an eagerness to apply his learnings. He knew that the journey ahead would be filled with challenges, but he also knew that he was now better equipped to face them.

DAY 3
A Quiet Clearing

LUCAS AWOKE TO THE RAYS OF DAWN CASTING A soft glow through the fabric of his yurt. He stretched, feeling a peaceful anticipation for the day ahead. As he stepped outside, expecting to head towards the communal dining area for breakfast, he found a surprising sight at his doorstep: a tray full of beautifully arranged food, surrounded by fresh flowers, and accompanied by a note.

After bringing the tray inside, Lucas picked up the note. It read:

Dear Lucas,

Good morning! I hope this breakfast brings warmth and joy as you start your day.
Today, I want to share with you a powerful lesson I learned from Isaac, one that has deeply influenced my practice and understanding of coaching and life itself.

Isaac often spoke about the power of silence and described it as a rich, fertile ground for awareness and transformation. He taught me that silence is not

*something to be filled or avoided but embraced as a
sacred space where true awareness can surface.*

*In silence, we embody a state of being that is
markedly different from any active state. It is in this
sacred stillness that we allow ourselves to truly
listen, not only to the words of others but to the
voice within us.*

*Silence is a gift we give ourselves and others. It
offers us a chance to be present, to connect deeply
without the need for words. So, today, I challenge
you to practice embracing silence. Find moments
throughout your day to be silent with yourself and
with anyone you encounter. Notice how this practice
affects your state of being, your interactions, and
the space it creates for awareness to emerge.*

*Remember, in the silence, we often find the answers
we've been seeking, within the quietude of our own
hearts.*

With warmth and silence,

Marina

Lucas read the note twice, letting the message sink in.
The challenge to embrace silence resonated with him,
especially after the realizations of the past days. With a sense
of reverence, he took a moment to appreciate the breakfast
and flowers.

As he ate, he reflected on Marina's words and Isaac's
lesson, pondering how he could integrate silence into his day.
He decided to approach the day's activities with a mindful
presence, intentionally seeking moments of silence, both in
solitude and in interactions with others.

As Lucas absorbed the tranquility of the morning and the thought-provoking challenge set before him, memories of an old meditation course he'd once taken surfaced. The instructor had emphasized that meditation was indeed a practice, a continuous journey towards stillness and clarity, not a destination to be perfected. This insight brought a feeling of ease to Lucas, softening the apprehension that bubbled up at the thought of embracing more silence in his interactions.

He acknowledged to himself that silence, especially in conversations, often felt like an uncomfortable void, one that he, like many, instinctively rushed to fill with words. This realization prompted him to revisit the fundamentals of his meditation practice, to reacquaint himself with the comfort and clarity that silence could offer before he ventured into the day's encounters.

After breakfast, Lucas found a peaceful spot, a quiet nook where the only sounds were the soft rustle of leaves and the orchestra of birds singing. He settled into a comfortable sitting position, closed his eyes, and took a deep, steadying breath, preparing to immerse himself in silence.

He remembered the analogy his meditation teacher had used, comparing the mind in meditation to a glass of freshly squeezed lemonade. Just as the pulp eventually settles to the bottom when left undisturbed, so too would his thoughts and the incessant internal chatter quiet down, allowing clarity and calm to emerge.

With this imagery in mind, Lucas committed to spending the next ten minutes in silent meditation. It was a manageable goal, one he felt confident he could achieve. As he began to focus on his breath, letting the inhales and exhales anchor him in the present moment, Lucas gradually felt the initial discomfort of silence begin to dissipate.

Minute by minute, the mental noise that had clouded his mind started to settle, much like the pulp in the lemonade analogy. The urge to fill the silence with activity or thought lessened, replaced by an emerging sense of peace. In this space of stillness, Lucas found connection—to himself, to the moment, and to the environment around him.

When Lucas opened his eyes, he felt refreshed and grounded. The stillness, far from being unsettling, was actually comforting. It dawned on him that this was a practice he needed more of in his life—to really understand and become comfortable with silence. So today, he decided, would be dedicated to embracing that silence fully. No interactions, no conversations, just him and the sounds of the island.

Lucas left his yurt, determined to embark on a solitary trek through the island's lush forest. The path he chose was known for its breathtaking natural beauty, a place where the dense, green canopy seemed to hum with a life of its own. His goal was clear: to walk in silence, to truly listen and absorb the world around him without the interference of his usual internal dialogue.

Shortly after he stepped into the forest, Lucas felt a shift. The world seemed to open up in a way he hadn't noticed before. The rustle of leaves underfoot, the distant calls of birds, the gentle caress of the wind—all these elements came into sharp focus, each sound and sensation amplified by the quietude.

With each step, Lucas calmed the chatter in his mind, bringing his attention back to the present moment. It was a struggle at first; his thoughts rebelled, seeking to fill the silence with the familiar noise of worries, plans, and reflections. But gradually, as he continued to walk, a deep level of listening began to take over. The natural symphony of the forest offered a richness and depth he had never truly appreciated.

In this state of heightened awareness, Lucas encountered a profound insight. The silence he had once sought to escape was actually teeming with life, not a void to be feared or filled. He realized that in stepping back from his own narratives, he had found a deeper connection to the nature around him and to his own inner self.

As Lucas wandered through the forest, his path led him to the gentle murmurs of a babbling brook. The sound, both calming and persistent, invited him to pause and truly listen—a fitting continuation of his day's silent exploration. Spotting a large rock beside the water, he decided to settle and immerse himself further into the natural surroundings.

The rock, while offering a vantage point, was far from ideal for sitting, its hard surface pressing against him in a way that was less than comfortable.

As Lucas settled into this spot, the initial ease brought on by the soothing sounds of the brook was gradually overshadowed by the growing discomfort of the rock. He tried shifting, attempting to find a position that might offer some relief, but each adjustment only brought temporary respite. The temptation to stand and relieve the discomfort was strong, an almost reflexive response to the unpleasant sensation.

It was then that a realization dawned on him. This physical discomfort, though minor, mirrored the emotional and psychological discomfort he often felt in moments of prolonged silence. Just as he was now resisting the urge to move away from the rock, he recognized the importance of resisting the urge to fill the silence in conversations. The discomfort, whether physical or mental, wasn't something to be avoided but rather embraced as part of the process.

Lucas chose to stay seated on the rock, to lean into the discomfort rather than escape it. He likened this to the practice he wanted to cultivate of sitting in the discomfort of silence with his clients, understanding that this was an opportunity for growth and for facilitating a space where true insight could emerge.

As he acknowledged the pain rising from the hard surface beneath him, Lucas allowed himself a small smile. This was an experiment in silence, but also a tangible practice in embracing discomfort for the sake of deeper learning. He focused back on the sound of the water, the discomfort becoming a secondary concern to the peacefulness of the moment.

This silly experiment, as he termed it, was a poignant reminder of the power of silence and the lessons that can emerge from the most mundane of circumstances. Lucas found a surprising depth of understanding in this moment of discomfort by the brook, a lesson he was eager to carry with him.

As Lucas stood up to leave, a thought struck him. "Why do I always feel the need to fill the silence? What makes silence so uncomfortable for me?" He mulled over these questions, recognizing a potential area for growth. There was definitely something to uncover, a block that, if addressed, could make embracing silence easier. Maybe, he thought, understanding this could help him become more comfortable with the pauses that were so essential in deep listening.

◆

Lucas's walk back to the retreat site was accompanied by the gentle grumbling of his stomach. As he approached the dining area, he was immediately faced with a decision: to maintain his practice of silence by dining alone or to join the lively group of fellow participants. His contemplation was cut short by Brandon's enthusiastic greeting, beckoning him over to a table filled with inviting faces.

Lucas made his way to the table, internally committed to extending his practice of silence into this social setting. As he settled into the rhythm of the group's dialogue, he found himself particularly drawn to Tina's passionate declaration of her struggle with the day's challenge. Tina, a fifty-year-old life coach with a vibrant New York accent, vividly described her discomfort with silence. She attributed it to her Italian heritage where lively, overlapping conversations were the norm. Her confession that silence felt almost alien to her sparked a familiar urge in Lucas to share his own feelings and insights. However, mindful of his commitment to practice silence, Lucas chose to listen attentively, offering nods and understanding glances instead of words. He recognized this as a moment to apply what he had learned during the retreat so far - to genuinely believe in the person's ability to arrive at their own answer, to inquire about their internal world versus their external actions, and of course to appreciate the value of silence.

Eventually when Tina paused, searching for confirmation or rebuttal from her audience, Lucas saw an opening not to break his silence with his story but to deepen the conversation with a thoughtful question. He leaned forward and asked, "Tina, what does it feel like when you sit in silence?" The idea that he was asking Tina the question he himself needed to answer was not lost on him.

Tina hesitated for a moment, then, with wide eyes, replied, "Like I want to jump out of my skin. It feels like wasted time. Awkward, you know?" Her voice conveyed frustration, a sentiment that Lucas could relate to.

Seeing an opening to explore deeper, Lucas asked, "What might be beneath that feeling of awkwardness and wasted time?"

Tina seemed caught off guard by the question. "I'm not sure, I haven't really thought about it," she admitted.

Lucas felt the urge to offer her an answer like, "Is it possible that silence could be offering you something, like an opportunity to learn or reflect?" But he resisted.

Instead, he let his original question hang in the air for a moment longer, allowing Tina to ponder a perspective she hadn't considered before. After a few more seconds she said, "I suppose I've always viewed silence as something to be filled, ...not as a space that could be full already," she slowly conceded.

"Hmmm. That's so interesting. ...And if silence were to be full of something, what do you think it could be full of?" Lucas gently probed.

Tina paused, the idea taking root. "Um... I don't know... clarity? Or a chance to listen to what's usually drowned out, maybe?"

Encouraged by her openness, Lucas left Tina with one more question to deepen her reflection, "How might viewing silence in this way change the way you feel about it?"

Tina's initial resistance began to soften as she considered Lucas's questions. Though still uncertain, she was now curious about the potential silence held for insight, a stark contrast to her earlier disdain.

The conversation, guided solely by Lucas's thoughtful inquiries, allowed Tina to confront her discomfort with silence and consider its value. Lucas, adhering to the day's challenge, left feeling affirmed that he could facilitate a meaningful interaction without imposing his views, demonstrating the true impact of curiosity-driven engagement and the power of silence.

◆

As Lucas allowed the rest of the afternoon to unfold in quiet contemplation, the insights from the day began to crystallize. The silence that had once seemed so elusive, now felt like a teacher, revealing layers of understanding.

Reflecting on his conversation with Tina, Lucas acknowledged a newfound clarity in his approach. It dawned on him that the serenity he experienced during his silent walk and meditation directly contributed to his ability to navigate the conversation with more depth and presence. The absence of his usual internal chatter made room for Tina's words and enabled him to listen with an openness he hadn't fully realized was possible.

This sparked an idea that felt revolutionary. Lucas considered the potential of integrating deliberate moments of silence into his daily routine, especially before coaching sessions. The constant rush from one appointment to the next, with scarcely a moment to breathe, suddenly appeared as an oversight rather than a necessity.

"Why haven't I done this before?" he pondered. Preparing for meetings, presentations, and even personal events with due diligence was second nature to him. Yet, applying the same level of preparation to create a mental and emotional clearing before sessions was a novel concept.

The quiet day had offered Lucas more than just a respite from the noise; it had provided a blueprint for enhancing his coaching practice. By carving out space for silence before each session, he could ensure that he approached every interaction with the clarity and presence necessary to facilitate meaningful change.

The sun set, and as Lucas prepared to turn in for the night, he felt a sense of gratitude for the day's challenge. Embracing silence had deepened his understanding of its value in coaching and illuminated a path to becoming a more effective coach.

Lying in bed, Lucas quietly made a commitment to himself: "I will consciously incorporate more space for silence in my life. This will be my best practice for preparing for coaching sessions too—creating a mind that is open, clear, and ready to receive whatever my clients bring to the table." Satisfied with this and tired from the day's revelations, Lucas drifted off with a peaceful feeling in his heart.

DAY 4

Echo Valley

THE MORNING AIR WAS FILLED WITH ANTICIPATION as the retreat participants gathered for breakfast. Marina opened the floor for reflections on the previous day's challenge: "Who would like to share their revelations or learnings about embracing silence?"

Elizabeth was the first to share. "I realized something interesting about silence; it's a pause in the conversation that allows space for deeper understanding to emerge," she began. "Allowing for silence in my interactions showed me that both I and the person I'm speaking with can learn so much more."

Lucas, carrying the quiet confidence of yesterday's revelations, nodded in agreement before adding his perspective. "One thing I discovered was the importance of preparation. Spending time in silence before interacting with others cleared my mind in ways I hadn't anticipated. It allowed me to approach each conversation with more attentiveness."

Tina, whose initial resistance to the challenge had been vocal, surprised herself with her takeaway. "I never thought I'd say this, but I learned that silence doesn't have to be my enemy. It's uncomfortable, and I think it's because I'm avoiding some things, ya know? It's not gonna be easy, but it's something I want to explore."

Marina listened intently, her eyes reflecting understanding. "Each of your experiences," she said, "highlights a unique aspect of silence. All these are invaluable lessons in both coaching and life."

Marina continued, "Silence is a powerful tool. It's a space where growth, reflection, and transformation can occur. Embrace silence, and you'll find it has much to teach you."

The breakfast conversation, rich with shared revelations, underscored the incredible power of the retreat's challenges. Each participant had uncovered aspects of themselves that would influence their paths long after the retreat had ended.

After breakfast, Marina gathered everyone for what she promised would be a memorable journey. "Today, I'm going to share a special place with you all, and it is there that we'll embrace our challenge for the day," she announced.

The group set out, leaving the familiar grounds of the retreat behind. Their path wound through low brush, over gentle hills, and across the babbling brook Lucas sat beside the day before. Each step took them deeper into the heart of the island's beauty. The terrain challenged them, coaxing beads of sweat and breaths of exertion as they navigated the landscape.

Twenty minutes later, the group crested the final hill, and the terrain opened up to a breathtaking valley that stretched out before them. Marina allowed everyone a moment to take in the vista.

"This," Marina said, turning to face the group, "is Echo Valley." Her voice carried a reverence fitting for the introduction of a sacred space. "For generations, this has been a place where truth is spoken, and truth is heard. It's not just the echoes that make this place special—it's the clarity and awareness that they bring back to us."

The participants, now fully captivated, exchanged curious glances. Marina explained that Echo Valley was known for its unique acoustic properties, where one's voice, when directed northward, would return with astonishing clarity.

"To demonstrate," Marina pivoted to face north and spoke into the valley. "Our truth must not be lost on us." Her words sailed through the air, reaching into the depths of the valley, and then, as promised, returned to them with such clarity it was as though the valley itself was speaking.

A collective gasp rippled through the group. Marina smiled at their reaction, pleased to see the valley's magic at work.

She addressed the group, "As you may know, mirroring the thoughts and feelings expressed by others can add clarity or emphasis to what they've said. So, today," she continued, "your challenge is to use reflection as a tool to hold up truth and build awareness for others. But first, you must experience this yourself, firsthand."

She guided them to spread out along the edge of the valley facing north, ensuring each person had their own space to witness the echo. "Try it," she urged. "Speak your truths into the valley. Wait for them to return to you and really listen to the echo of your words."

One by one, the participants spoke their truths into Echo Valley. They spoke of fears, aspirations, and discoveries, each phrase returned to them with a clarity that seemed to give their words weight and significance. It was an exercise in vulnerability and courage, as speaking one's truth aloud, to be clearly echoed back, was a moving experience.

The exercise was more than just a physical demonstration of an echo; it was a metaphorical journey into the value of reflection. Lucas and the others were beginning to understand how reflecting someone's words back to them could validate their feelings and thoughts and give them space to be present with their value.

At the end of the session, the group gathered together to share their revelations; and the trek back to the retreat site was filled with deep contemplation, each person internally processing the lessons of Echo Valley.

Marina, walking among them, felt a sense of accomplishment. "The echoes we heard today," she reminded them, "are echoes of truth, understanding, and connection. I invite you to carry this lesson with you in your practice as coaches and leaders, as well as in every conversation you have."

After a day filled with serene beauty and the special time at Echo Valley, the retreat participants reconvened in the early evening at a pavilion near the beach. As the sun dipped lower, Marina introduced the evening's activity, an exercise in reflective listening and mirroring.

As Marina arranged the participants in a small circle, Lucas took his place, the ocean breeze grounding him in the present moment. He listened intently as Marina outlined the exercise: each person would share a story or insight, and the person directly across from them would act as a mirror by reflecting back the words spoken. No need to ask questions. Just reflection. Marina's guidance focused on the power of listening to understand, to truly hear, and then to mirror back another's words without interjection or interpretation...and for the purposes of this activity, without inquiry.

Brandon spoke up, "What do you mean without inquiry?" He looked at Marina inquisitively. "Like no questions at all?"

"Yes," she nodded. "Trust me."

Lucas was particularly attuned to the potential of this exercise. Reflective listening and mirroring were skills he recognized as crucial to his growth as a coach. But his curiosity was piqued by the idea of not asking questions at all.

Lucas looked forward to engaging with Natalia, his partner for the exercise, and to exploring the depth of understanding that lay in the spaces filled by reflections in place of questions.

Natalia began by sharing her story with vulnerability, touching on her challenges in navigating the complexities of leadership.

"As an entrepreneur and manager of many contractors, I'm constantly juggling assertiveness with empathy in my leadership position," she started, her eyes scanning the attentive faces. "It feels like I'm either too harsh or too soft, never striking the right balance. It's like walking a tightrope without a safety net," she confessed.

Lucas, eager to employ reflective techniques, waited for Natalia to complete her thoughts before responding. "You're feeling torn," he echoed, "between being too harsh or too soft. That sounds incredibly challenging, trying to strike the right balance...as if you were walking on a tightrope."

Natalia nodded, encouraged by the acknowledgement. "Exactly. And it's like, no matter what I do, I end up questioning my decisions, wondering if I could have been more effective in another way."

"You end up questioning your decisions," Lucas reflected. "It seems you're in a constant state of wondering if there was a more effective way."

"Yes, that's it," Natalia confirmed, "I want to lead with confidence and empathy, to be a beacon for my team, but it's hard when I'm doubting myself."

"You want to lead with confidence...and empathy," Lucas reiterated slowly, giving space to each of Natalia's aspirations. "Being a beacon for your team is important to you, ...but the self-doubt makes it hard."

Natalia paused, taking in Lucas's reflections, each one shedding light on her internal dialogue. "Hmm... it makes me realize that maybe it's not about finding a perfect balance but accepting the flux. Maybe it's okay to lean more into one side as the situation demands."

"So, you're saying it might not be about finding a perfect balance but accepting the flux," Lucas repeated, his voice gentle yet clear. "Leaning more into one side as the situation demands... might be a new way of seeing it. Is that right?"

Natalia's expression softened, "Yes, and I think that accepting this flux could actually be my strength, not a weakness. I can be both assertive and empathetic, depending on what my team needs."

"Accepting this flux...could be your strength," Lucas mirrored back. "Being both assertive and empathetic ...depending on your team's needs."

"Yes! That's right." Natalia sounded both certain and excited. "This feels like a real shift in perspective. Exactly what I needed. Thanks so much, Lucas!"

The group broke out in applause and Lucas felt his face blush. "You're welcome, but I didn't do anything, Natalia. It was all you!"

As the applause concluded Marina looked toward Lucas, her expression filled with approval.

"Lucas," she began, "that was a remarkable example of the power of reflective listening. You created a space for Natalia to explore her own thoughts and feelings in a way that led her to new insights and self-understanding."

Marina continued, "Your approach—deliberate, methodical, and deeply respectful—allowed Natalia to hear her own words in a new light. It was a beautiful demonstration of how supportive reflection can be."

"Lucas" she asked, "What did you notice about that interaction with Natalia?"

Marina's inquiry prompted Lucas to reflect deeper on his approach during the exercise. "I was very intentional about how I echoed Natalia's words back to her," Lucas shared, a note of realization in his voice. "I made sure to repeat them slowly, giving each word space and weight. And I was so present with her words that I didn't feel pressure to come up with a question. I used the space I had to hold up the mirror so she could recognize her own wisdom."

Marina listened intently, nodding in agreement at his insights. "That level of presence you're describing, Lucas, is exactly what turns a good coach into a great one," she remarked. "You've tapped into something essential here— the power of truly being with someone in their moment of sharing, without the rush to 'fix' or 'solve.'"

She emphasized her next point, "And this space you mentioned, the absence of pressure to immediately respond with a question, that's the cradle of insight. In those moments of silence, of simply being and reflecting, you're holding up a mirror for Natalia and inviting her into a deeper conversation with herself."

Tina, unable to hold her skepticism any longer, cut in with a pointed observation. "But wait a minute," she began, her voice tinged with frustration, "If I started doing that with my clients, they would just look at me and say, 'Polly wanna cracker?'"

Marina looked puzzled. "Polly?" she echoed, seeking clarification.

"Yeah, because I'd sound like a parrot, just repeating everything they say!" she exclaimed, her hands gesturing for emphasis. The room broke into chuckles and nods of agreement.

Marina, now fully grasping Tina's concern, smiled warmly. "I see what you're saying, Tina. The last thing we want is to sound like we're mimicking without adding value. It's a fine line between reflective listening and feeling like we're just repeating words without purpose."

Elizabeth, catching onto the thread of the conversation, added her perspective on the role of questions in coaching. "I've always leaned heavily on questions to dig deeper. It's like...without them, am I even coaching?"

Marina smiled at the engagement. "Both of you are touching on crucial aspects of coaching. Reflection, as Lucas showcased, serves to mirror the person's thoughts and emotions, offering them a chance to hear their words from another perspective. It's not about being a parrot but providing a space for them to be present with their own wisdom. Questions, on the other hand, guide them to explore further. Using both, strategically, enhances the coaching conversation."

Seeing an opportunity for a more practical application, Marina proposed another round of the exercise, again with Natalia, but this time integrating questions with reflections. Elizabeth eagerly volunteered, ready to apply the dual approach.

As Natalia began, she revisited her challenges with leadership, specifically her quest for the right balance between assertiveness and empathy. "I want to act like I have command, but I don't want to isolate myself from the team members." Elizabeth listened intently, before speaking. "So, you're striving to lead with authority while keeping the human connection with your team," Elizabeth reflected, capturing the essence of Natalia's struggle. "Does that sound accurate?"

"Yes, exactly," Natalia responded, visibly pleased to be understood.

Marina jumped in, "Masterfully done, Elizabeth! Adding the clarifying question after your reflection was the right thing to do there. When we reflect using different words than those spoken, we must check in with the person to see if we have captured the true meaning." Marina gestured toward Elizabeth, "Continue, please."

Elizabeth then introduced a question, aiming to deepen the exploration. "What moments have you felt that balance was just right?" she inquired.

Natalia paused, considering her experiences. "Well, there was a project last quarter where I felt I really nailed it," she began. "We were under a lot of pressure, and I managed to stay calm and assertive. I made sure to listen carefully to everyone's input, which made my team feel valued."

Elizabeth encouraged Natalia to explore deeper. "How did maintaining that balance between calm and assertive make you feel about your leadership style?" she asked.

"It felt empowering," Natalia admitted. "Not just for me, but for the whole team. We achieved excellent results because everyone felt involved and important."

"It felt empowering," Elizabeth reflected. "Not just for you, ...but for the whole team. And everyone felt involved and important."

Giving space for the reflection to sink in with Natalia, "It sounds like you created an environment where empathy amplified your authority," Elizabeth reflected, tying back to their initial discussion. "What comes up for you as you hear that?"

Natalia paused to take that in. "I think that may be true, although I had never considered that before." Gazing upward for a few seconds before continuing, "I guess I need to remember that my empathy doesn't undermine my authority—it actually strengthens it."

"Ah," said Elizabeth. "Your empathy doesn't *undermine* your authority...it actually *strengthens* it." Feeding back Natalia's words like small spoonful's of chocolate pudding. "How does that feel?"

"Pretty darn good!" Natalia replied through a big smile.

Marina nodded approvingly as the group absorbed the demonstration. "Excellent work, Elizabeth," she affirmed, addressing the group with a tone of enthusiasm. "What we've just seen is a prime example of skillfully blending reflection with questioning to create awareness. Elizabeth's approach of checking in with Natalia throughout the discussion was masterfully done. This ensures we don't impose our interpretations on others, but rather help them explore their own thoughts and feelings."

Marina continued, her voice carrying an air of passion. "Our role isn't to provide our interpretation but to guide others in uncovering their own. The questions Elizabeth used—'Does that sound accurate?', 'What comes up for you as you hear that?', and 'How does that feel?'— invite people to engage deeply, reflect on their situation, and own their insights."

She gestured broadly. "This is where the art and science of coaching intersects. It's not merely about the tools we choose but how we apply them to foster connection, understanding, and ultimately, empowerment. Masterful coaching involves this dynamic interplay where we adapt our approach to meet people exactly where they are and help them move forward."

Marina paused, letting her words resonate with the group. "Keep practicing this," she encouraged. "Integrate it into your conversations and watch how it can improve your interactions with others."

Feeling like he wanted to contribute to the conversation, Brandon chimed in. "That was awesome Elizabeth! I have a question though," looking toward Marina, "would this kind of reflection work if the client wasn't saying something smart—but instead something weird or crazy?"

Brandon's question sparked interest, and the group was eager for her insight. "That's an excellent question, Brandon," Marina acknowledged. "And I have a personal experience that might just shed some light on this."

She took a moment to gather her thoughts, her gaze drifting as if she were visualizing the scene she was about to recount. "When I first arrived at the island, I found myself in a rather negative state of mind. I was caught up in a whirlwind of self-doubt and criticism about my job and my life in general," Marina began. "Then, I met Isaac who immediately sensed my turmoil and decided it was a good idea to introduce me to Echo Valley."

She described how Isaac led her to the valley under the guise of an exercise that would help her see her situation in a new light. "He asked me to face north and voice all the negativity I was feeling, all the doubts and fears. I thought maybe hearing them out loud in that sacred space would transform them somehow," Marina said.

"But the valley did what it does best—it echoed back my words exactly as I had spoken them. Hearing my own negativity repeated back to me was jarring. It wasn't the enlightening experience I had expected. Instead, it was a stark reflection of the pessimism I was allowing to dominate my thoughts."

Marina paused, allowing the weight of her story to sink in. "That visit to Echo Valley was a turning point for me. It made me acutely aware of how my words—negative or otherwise—affect my own mindset, and also how they might affect others around me."

"The lesson here," Marina concluded, "is not that we should only echo back the 'smart' things people say. It's that sometimes, by mirroring their words—no matter how 'weird' or negative—they might hear themselves differently. It's about awareness, about helping them see their own thoughts and feelings from a new perspective, much like Echo Valley did for me."

The group absorbed Marina's story, the lesson profound. It was a reminder of the power of reflection as a means of fostering self-awareness.

A short while later, the session ended, and it was clear to Marina that the group was leaving with a deeper appreciation for the positive effects of combining reflective listening with thoughtful questioning.

Lucas, heading back to his yurt, felt a sense of clarity from this exercise as it had deepened his appreciation for the subtleties of masterful coaching.

As Lucas settled into bed that night, the reality that the retreat was more than half over hit him. Realizing he hadn't made any entries in his journal—a goal he'd set at the beginning—he reached for the leather-bound book beside his bed. Opening to a fresh page, he began to jot down his thoughts from the day's learning:

Today was a great reminder of the power of words and their role in shaping our understanding of ourselves. I've learned that our clients don't just need us to ask questions; sometimes, our role is to simply mirror their own words back to them. Reflecting on what they say can help them see their own insights more clearly. It struck me that we might miss critical moments of transformation if we overlook the chance to reflect their thoughts, beliefs, and brilliance back to them. I want to focus on using reflections more thoughtfully in my sessions, balancing them with questions to deepen my clients' awareness.

After penning his reflections, Lucas closed his journal and settled into bed. The rhythmic sounds of the island night soothed him as he drifted off into a contemplative sleep.

DAY 5
Beyond the Rain

THE NEXT MORNING, LUCAS AWOKE TO THE rhythmic tapping of rain on his yurt's roof. "Island weather," he mused, his enthusiasm dampened by the sudden change in weather.

Shielding himself under the canopy of palms, Lucas made his way to the indoor dining area. The retreat participants were already queued at the buffet. The atmosphere, usually vibrant and animated, was subdued under the gray skies.

Once everyone was seated, Marina began, noting the palpable shift in the group's energy. "It seems there's been a distinct change in our energy and mood today, different from yesterday. Does that resonate with you?" she inquired. The room, filled with silent nods, confirmed her observation.

Natalia quickly added, "Yes, it's a noticeable shift, isn't it? Quite different from the previous days."

"What do you think that might be about?" Marina probed further.

Tina, ever the straightforward one, quipped, "It's pretty obvious, just look outside!"

Natalia suggested, "It's the rain and lack of sunlight. It's so dreary out."

"Interesting, what else might be contributing?" Marina encouraged.

Brandon sheepishly confessed, "I started the day feeling pretty good, but somehow, being here, I felt my energy dip, feeding off the group's vibe."

Marina continued, "How would you each describe your current mood or energy?"

The responses varied greatly— Brandon felt "low," Elizabeth found the day "cozy and sleepy," Lucas admitted to feeling "lazy," Tina confessed to a sense of "depression," and Natalia could only describe her mood as "different."

Marina nodded, absorbing their words. "Interesting. Thank you for sharing."

Transitioning to a teaching moment, Marina asked, "Ok, so what did I model there that might be helpful in your coaching?"

Tina spoke first, "You detected that the rain put us all in a foul mood without us even saying a word."

Marina clarified, "I noted a shift in energy, yes, but I didn't specifically blame the rain nor label the mood as 'foul'. Elizabeth?"

"You observed the change and checked in to see if we felt it too." Elizabeth added.

"And then?" Marina encouraged.

"You inquired about our own interpretations of this shift," Lucas noted, catching on.

"Right. While I might've guessed the rain played a part, I kept my assumptions at bay and sought your perspectives instead," Marina explained.

"What followed?" she pressed on.

"You invited us to describe our feelings," Brandon noted, visibly excited.

"That's correct," Marina said. "I didn't presume to know your emotions. Had I done so, considering your varied responses, I could've misinterpreted them."

She concluded, "This illustrates three key lessons. First, effective listening goes beyond words to the unspoken, sensing and observing changes in energy or mood. Second, we share observations without asserting them as truths, inviting others to confirm. And third, we refrain from assuming or labeling the causes of the shift or the emotions they are provoking, choosing to inquire instead."

The group absorbed the multiple lessons, albeit a bit amused by how many can result from just a few minutes of interaction.

"Alright, let's move forward," Marina said, eager to maintain the momentum of discovery. "This activity will help you practice listening, beyond the words and beyond the immediate." She smiled, anticipation lighting up her face, as she prepared the group for an exploration into the depths of masterful listening.

Marina began, "I'd like you all to close your eyes and listen intently. Then I will ask you to open your eyes and share your observations." The room quieted down, everyone closed their eyes, their focus sharpened in the absence of visual distractions.

After a few seconds, Marina asked them to share what they heard. The group collectively answered "rain". Marina pushed further and asked, "Why do you think you could only hear the rain?"

Lucas chimed in, "I think it's because it's the loudest of all sounds, like the noise in the foreground. Is that it?" Marina acknowledged his answer with a nod before continuing.

"Ok, now close your eyes and listen again. What else can you hear, beyond the rain?"

Encouraged to deepen their listening, the group's awareness expanded, unveiling the symphony that existed alongside the rainfall—birds chirping, wind whistling, palm leaves rustling, kitchen activity, and the distant ocean—all coexisting with the rain but unnoticed until that moment.

As Marina guided everyone's attention beyond the immediate, she was illustrating a vital coaching skill: the ability to listen not just to what is being said in the foreground with words, but also to what is lurking in the background, the unspoken or unnoticed.

"This," Marina emphasized, "is where the art of deep listening lies. The skill of tuning into the subtler frequencies can reveal a lot about a person's internal state or untapped awareness. These elements, though seemingly minor, can hold the keys to deeper understanding and breakthroughs...and we must train ourselves to listen for them."

Marina continued, "Isaac would often say that sometimes the loudest truths are those unvoiced." Marina paused to let the idea sink in. "By listening at multiple levels, you can support people in exploring what they are expressing through words, but also the deeper truths that lie beneath...truths they may not even be aware of. And this," she stressed, "is the depth of listening we're aiming for."

"So, your challenge today is to practice multiple levels of listening. As you go about your day, tune into the entirety of what's being communicated—not only to what is in the forefront, but also to what might be in the background. Listen with your ears, your eyes, and your heart. Sense shifts in energy, body language, pauses, and anything else that might be a clue to what people are communicating without words."

"Oh," she added, "and be sure to enjoy the process."

◆

Motivated by Marina's demonstration, Lucas ventured forth, eager to apply this learning.

It wasn't long before Lucas stumbled upon an unexpected opportunity to deepen his practice of listening at different levels. The local community was hosting an event in the town square to showcase the high school students' projects on various environmental themes. This setting, vibrant with voices and bustling with activity, provided Lucas with a diverse arena to apply the nuanced listening skills he was cultivating.

As Lucas meandered through the displays, absorbing the creativity and passion poured into each project, he was drawn to a small crowd gathered around a presentation on efforts to preserve the island's unique biodiversity. The presenter, a girl named Ana, was animatedly discussing her findings, her voice fluctuating with a blend of excitement and trepidation.

He observed Ana closely, noting her words but also the wealth of non-verbal cues she was unconsciously offering. Her hands fluttered with enthusiasm as she spoke about the coral reefs, yet they clenched slightly when she mentioned the threats they faced. Her eyes sought out her teacher's face, searching for reassurance, whenever she stumbled over her words. These subtle signs spoke volumes to Lucas, revealing Ana's deep commitment to her subject and her underlying anxiety about conveying its importance effectively.

After her presentation, Lucas approached Ana to congratulate her on her work. As they engaged in conversation, Lucas made a conscious effort to listen deeply to Ana's words and also to the entire context of her communication. He paid attention to her body language, the pauses filled with thought or uncertainty, the sighs of relief when he showed genuine interest, and the way her posture relaxed as she realized her message was being received.

"Ana, that was an exceptional presentation. Your commitment to revive the island's preservation methods is incredibly moving," he offered warmly, hoping to convey his genuine admiration.

"Thank you, sir," Ana replied, her tone carrying a sliver of uncertainty.

"Oh, sorry. My name's Lucas. It's nice to meet you." Ana smiled warmly as Lucas continued. "How did it feel up there sharing your ideas with the community?"

"It felt ok, I guess. It's always a bit nerve-wracking, wondering if others will see the value in what feels so personal to me."

Noticing the quick, tentative glance she cast towards her notes, Lucas inquired gently, "What made you the most nervous?" he.

Ana hesitated, her fingers tracing the edges of her presentation materials. "I suppose I feared the reaction to blending so much of our ancient culture with today's. There's a delicate line there, and I wasn't sure I'd walked it correctly."

Observing her careful choice of words and the earnest concern reflected in her gestures, Lucas realized the depth of her commitment. "Hmm. From my perspective that's exactly what makes your work so vital. You're acting as a bridge between times. How does it feel to immerse yourself in your ancestors' beliefs and methodology?"

As she spoke of her deep connection to the island's past, her body language shifted from tentative to animated. "Honestly, it feels like coming home. Like I am reconnecting with a part of me I didn't realize was missing." Her voice grew more assured as she shared her experience. "It's almost as if I'm uncovering hidden chapters of my own story," Ana admitted, a newfound vibrancy in her voice.

Lucas, keenly observing the nuances of their interaction, wanted to bridge the gap between what was said and what remained unspoken. "Ana, I'm curious—how does it feel to discuss your personal ties to the island's heritage?" he inquired.

Ana paused, her expression contemplative. After a moment, she responded, "Actually, talking about my passion for island preservation from the perspective of those who came before me makes me feel...I don't know, more connected."

Encouraged by her self-awareness, Lucas shared his observation, "I notice a vivid shift in your energy as you speak about these connections, Ana. You seem to radiate with a kind of inner light. What do you think about that?"

Caught off guard by Lucas's reflection, Ana smiled, an enthusiastic glow in her eyes. "I didn't know it was that noticeable. I guess when I talk about my work, I feel more like myself. It's as if sharing my ancestors' stories rekindles a fire within me."

Lucas nodded, acknowledging her words, and coaxing her to continue.

"I hadn't fully realized it until now, but discussing my work and its roots stirs a passion in me that feels pretty amazing."

"Well," Lucas concluded, "it's beautiful to witness. It seems that your passion shapes your work and that's incredibly inspiring to me."

Ana thanked Lucas before asking him for a hug. She expressed her appreciation for their interaction and felt a strong sense of pride.

After parting ways, Lucas reflected on the brief interaction with Ana. This exchange offered him a clear example of the transformative power of listening at different levels—attuning to Ana's words but also to the shifts in her energy. It was a vivid reminder that true understanding often lies in the subtle expressions of our inner worlds made visible through genuine, attentive engagement. "What a wonderful rush!" Lucas mused to himself.

◆

After meandering through the town center for a while, Lucas suddenly found himself at the island's local market. The place was alive with the hum of vendors and shoppers, the air filled with the scents of local cuisine, and about a dozen or so stalls offered colorful produce and artifacts.

Amidst this sensory overload, Lucas' attention was drawn to a small stall in the corner of the market. The vendor, an elderly man with weathered hands and a warm smile, was displaying an array of handmade woodwork that spoke of the island's traditions. Each piece, from intricately carved totems to delicate bowls, was vibrant with stories waiting to be told. Lucas approached, drawn by a sense of genuine pride emanating from the man.

The craftsman, noticing Lucas's interest, began to share the history behind a striking carving of a bird mid-flight. "This bird," he said, his voice as textured as the wood he sculpted, "depicted with its wings outstretched in full represents freedom, resilience, and the enduring spirit of our community here," he explained, his fingers tracing the smooth lines of the bird's wings. "You see, the tree from which this was carved stood witness to countless storms, bearing the brunt of nature's fury, yet it remained steadfast, rooted deeply in the earth. Much like the bird, and indeed our people, it speaks to the power of facing challenges head-on and rising above them."

As Lucas listened, a sensation unlike any other took hold. The man's words, infused with the weight of history and meaning, stirred something deep within. It was a visceral reaction—a physical embodiment of the connection Lucas felt to the story being told.

The craftsman elaborated on the carving. "This bird, therefore, represents our ancestral strength and the unwavering belief in the possibility of new beginnings, of taking flight despite the odds."

Lucas, visibly affected by the craftsman's narrative, found his voice. "What you shared just sent a shiver through me," he confessed. "I can feel the depth and passion behind your words. Your craftsmanship, the stories it carries, it truly touches my heart and stirs hope in me."

The craftsman's eyes lit up with gratitude at Lucas's admission. "I've shared this story many times," he began, his voice carrying a note of reflection, "but hearing how it resonated with you gives it a new depth for me." He paused, considering his words. "Your response, your appreciation, it reinforces the value of what we pass down through generations. Thank you for sharing that with me."

"Thanks to you," replied Lucas, shaking the man's hand. "I really appreciate your passion and for sharing it so generously with me."

As the conversation concluded, both men felt a sense of satisfaction. The encounter had highlighted an important aspect of communication—when Lucas listened with his entire being and reflected his emotional response back to the craftsman, it enriched the exchange. This was a powerful realization: it wasn't just about hearing the words spoken, but also about tuning into his own reactions and sharing these insights. Then, this reflective sharing allowed the craftsman to see his impact and possibly gain a new perspective on his own narratives. "Incredible!" Lucas thought to himself.

———————◆———————

Later that evening, Lucas fished out his journal, wanting to keep his promise to himself to write every day. The pen felt eager in his hand, ready to record the lessons of the day. He wrote:

Today was really insightful for me. In the morning, Marina challenged us to listen at different levels, and said that masterful listening involves more than just hearing words; it's about connecting with the essence of what's being shared, sensing the emotion, the pauses, and the energy behind the spoken word.

Then a deep conversation with a highschooler named Ana helped me put this into action. I practiced listening to what she was saying, while also listening at an energetic level. I tried to look for those little signs that often go unnoticed. I noticed a shift in Ana's energy, and when I asked her about it, she connected to a deeper understanding of herself and her work. Amazing!

I'm more committed than ever to keep improving how I listen in my coaching sessions. I want to be there fully, hearing the words, feeling the emotions, and noticing those subtle cues that tell a deeper story.

Then, a brief encounter with a local craftsman at the market taught me that I can help people see and understand themselves better not only when I reflect back what I'm noticing about them, but also how their words and stories affect me. Sharing my own reactions seems to make the whole interaction more enlightening for them. That was kind of surprising.

I definitely want to bring this into my sessions. Today made it clear that this kind of deep listening and sharing can help people to see themselves more clearly.

I'm feeling pretty inspired to keep pushing forward with all of this and see where it can take my coaching skills.

Closing his journal, Lucas took a deep, soothing breath and drifted into a well-deserved slumber.

DAY 6

Hidden Treasures

LUCAS AWOKE TO THE FAMILIAR SOOTHING SOUNDS of nature—the ocean breeze, birds singing, and waves rolling into shore. Lying still for a moment, he let reality sink in: tomorrow he would be leaving this island retreat, heading back to the routine of his daily life. As he stretched, the fabric of the yurt rustled softly, a gentle reminder of how far from ordinary these past five days had been.

With a deep, contemplative sigh, Lucas sat up, his mind buzzing with the myriad of insights Marina had imparted. He thought about the challenges: believing in his clients more than himself, inquiring about the person's being before the doing, embracing the power of silence, using reflection to create awareness, and listening beyond the spoken words. Each lesson had opened new doors, revealing layers of complexity in the coaching process he had never fully appreciated before.

As he prepared for the day, Lucas's curiosity stirred. What could possibly top what they had already covered? The richness of the past lessons filled him with anticipation. Could there be more to learn that was as impactful as what had already been presented?

He made his way to the main pavilion, the path now familiar, almost comforting. The island had become more than just a place of learning; it was a sanctuary where he had discovered professional growth and personal revelations. Today, he felt ready, open to whatever the final day would unveil. What was left for Marina to offer? The thought lingered as he arrived at breakfast.

The retreat participants gathered in the outdoor dining area, their faces showing the fatigue and enlightenment that comes from deep personal work. As they settled around the tables laden with fresh tropical fruits and aromatic coffee, Marina stood to address the group.

"Good morning, everyone," Marina began, "today I will introduce the most crucial aspect of your ability to have a greater impact on others." She paused for effect. "Throughout this retreat, we've explored many important elements of coaching—trust and belief in others, deeper inquiry, silence, reflection, and listening on multiple levels. These are vital skills, but there's another important element, one that's often overlooked."

Marina smiled, her expression softening. "Isaac used to say, 'The true art of connection and support lies not only in the techniques we employ when we engage with others, but in the authenticity and heart we bring to each interaction.'

Today I invite you to consider that becoming a masterful coach and leader isn't just about perfecting your techniques but about integrating your personality, intuition, empathy, and humanity into the process."

The group listened intently, their faces reflecting slight surprise as they exchanged looks, but simultaneously recognizing the potential truth in her words.

"Think about it," Marina continued, "people aren't just looking for someone to ask the right questions or reflect back what they say. They're also looking for someone to connect with, someone who can see them and understand them on a human level. That's where you, with all your unique characteristics and qualities, come into play."

"Wait, what?" chimed Tina. "I remember learning in a master class that we were supposed to remove ourselves from the process, make it all about the client."

Marina acknowledged Tina's point with a thoughtful nod. "That's an excellent observation, Tina," she said. "In coaching, our role isn't to direct the conversation or impose our narratives or beliefs. But what masterful coaches do so well is bring to the table their intuition, empathy, vulnerability, and anything else that makes them human."

She allowed a brief pause before elaborating on the concept. "This balance is what elevates a coach from good to masterful. It's about knowing how to step back and let others navigate their path, while also being fully present and bringing your whole self into the session. Coaches early in their career struggle with this because they're so focused on the mechanics of learning a new skill."

Marina used an analogy to clarify her point. "Consider when you first learn to drive. You're hyper-focused on the technical aspects: handling the steering wheel, signaling turns, reading road signs. Your whole attention is on performing these actions correctly. But once you're proficient, driving becomes almost instinctual. You can relax and enjoy the journey, even converse with passengers. The same goes for coaching. Once you're confident with the fundamental techniques, you can truly relax into the role. That's when you're not just *doing* coaching; you're *being* a coach."

She scanned the room, ensuring the message resonated. "The transition from concentrating on the mechanics to simply being in the moment with someone is a significant leap. It marks the shift from mastering the *tools* of coaching to embodying the *spirit* of coaching." Marina's explanation aimed to illuminate the path from mastering technical skills to integrating personal authenticity in coaching.

Natalia was intrigued. She raised her hand and began to speak. "So, are you saying that we should bring our own feelings and experiences into the exchange?"

Marina nodded appreciatively at Natalia's question. "Yes, but the distinction is in *how* we engage with our own experiences and emotions in the coaching conversation."

She leaned slightly forward, her expression earnest. "It's important that everything we bring into the interaction serves the person's process. For instance, as a masterful coach, you wouldn't indulge in sharing your own struggles in great detail as a means of connection. Instead, you might briefly mention your experience to establish understanding, or you might share the emotions you feel as you listen to their struggles—not to center the conversation on yourself, but to deepen empathy and understanding."

This last statement made Lucas reflect on his interaction with the craftsman the day before. "That's kind of what I did." he thought to himself.

Marina paused to let her words sink in. "This dual approach allows us to maintain professional boundaries while also bringing our whole selves into coaching conversations. We are both a supportive presence and an authentic partner, helping illuminate their path without leading the way. That's the art of masterful coaching—it's about being present in a way that respects one's autonomy while also engaging our full humanity to foster a genuine connection."

She smiled warmly at Natalia. "Does that help clarify the balance we aim to strike?"

Natalia nodded and continued, "Yes, but it feels so different from what I've been doing thus far. I've worked so hard to take myself out of it, and now you're telling us to put ourselves back in. It seems like I have to unlearn in order to relearn."

Marina acknowledged Natalia's concern. "I understand how this might feel like a step backwards, Natalia, but think of it more as an expansion rather than a retraction of your skills," she explained.

"Early in your coaching journey, it's natural to focus heavily on the methodologies and the 'how-to'—like asking the right questions and following specific models. This is necessary because it builds a foundation. But as you grow, your role evolves. It's not about discarding those initial lessons but enriching them," Marina continued.

She gestured with her hands to emphasize her point. "Imagine it like adding layers to a painting. Initially, your canvas is about structure—the outline. As you progress, you start to add color and texture. Bringing your intuition, empathy, and realness into coaching conversations adds those deeper hues to your work."

Marina smiled reassuringly at the group. "It doesn't negate the importance of the basics you've learned; rather, it enhances them. You're not unlearning but integrating. You're learning to be both a guide and a fellow traveler. That's where true connection and transformation occur in coaching."

She concluded, "So yes, it might feel like relearning, but what you're really doing is deepening your practice. You're becoming adept at using all of your tools—both technical and personal—to meet people's needs more fully."

Marina's words seemed to strike a chord with the group. As she finished speaking, there was a thoughtful silence around the room. Participants exchanged glances, pondering the integration of their personal elements into their professional roles. It was clear that the idea of blending their authentic selves with their coaching techniques was a new concept for them.

Marina pressed on, "So, take a moment to consider—what feelings, characteristics, or personal experiences have you been keeping out of your coaching conversations? And how might bringing them in actually enrich your coaching?"

Marina's questions lingered in the air, prompting thoughtful introspection among the participants. After a pause, Natalia cleared her throat and spoke up. "For me, it's probably my intuition. I often have gut feelings, but I've held back, sticking strictly to the book. I'm now wondering if I could use my intuition to guide my questioning and make my interactions more impactful."

Elizabeth added, "I've always been a bit reserved, keeping my personal experiences separate from my coaching. I can imagine how sharing parts of my journey could help employees relate and open up more. It's about finding the right balance to connect on a human level without overshadowing their stories with mine."

Marina nodded approvingly at their insights. "Exactly," she affirmed, "integrating your intuition and personal experiences doesn't mean abandoning structure—it's about enriching the framework you already use. By weaving in your own instincts and stories where appropriate, you offer a richer, more empathetic connection. It's about enhancing the resonance of the interaction, not diluting it."

She continued, "Natalia, by trusting your gut, you allow your coaching to become more dynamic and responsive. And Elizabeth, by sharing relevant aspects of your journey, you model openness and trust, which are crucial in building strong relationships. Both approaches foster a deeper level of trust and safety."

Transitioning from the lesson to the application, Marina continued. "So, today, we're going to do something that I hope will enrich your understanding of how your personal experiences and professional roles can intersect in beautiful, often unexpected ways."

She paused to ensure she had everyone's attention. "We'll start with an independent walk around the island," Marina continued, gesturing towards the lush greenery surrounding them. "I want each of you to find a natural item during your walk. It could be anything—a shell, a stone, a leaf, a flower—something you feel a personal connection to or that you believe symbolizes a part of your personality, a challenge you've overcome, or a triumph you've celebrated. As you select your item, think about why it speaks to you. What story does it tell? How does it reflect who you are or what you've experienced?"

The group was visibly intrigued by Marina's proposal, exchanging smiles of anticipation. Marina then continued with her instructions. "When we return here," she indicated the circle of chairs, "you'll share your item and its meaning with the others."

With a nod, she concluded, "Ok, so open your hearts to the island, and find those items that speak to your souls. Meet back here in an hour, and we'll begin our sharing."

The group dispersed, energized by the prospect of discovery—not just of the island's natural treasures but also of deeper self-insight that would enhance their coaching.

◆

An hour later, the circle formed under the pavilion, with each participant holding their chosen symbol from nature.

Natalia was among the first to share. She held a smooth, rounded stone, its surface weathered by the elements. "I chose this stone because it reminds me of resilience," she began. "Several years ago, I endured a grueling battle with breast cancer. It was a storm that felt endless, testing my strength on every level—physically, emotionally, and spiritually." She paused, running her thumb over the stone's surface. "This stone, shaped and smoothed by the elements, symbolizes the resilience I discovered within myself. Despite the relentless challenges, I emerged stronger and more whole than before, much like how this stone remains intact despite its weathering."

After Natalia finished sharing, the circle fell into a respectful silence, each member processing the depth of her story. Elizabeth, who had been listening intently, found a connection to her own life experience.

Elizabeth sighed before speaking, her voice carrying empathy. "Natalia, thank you for sharing that. I can really relate. I went through a similar period of extreme challenge when I lost my sister to illness. It felt much like the storms you described shaping your stone."

Natalia's eyes met Elizabeth's with a sparkle of shared understanding. "Elizabeth, hearing you share that means so much to me. It's comforting to know others have walked through their own storms and come out stronger."

Lucas was next to share —holding up a large green leaf he had found. "This leaf represents renewal for me," he explained, lifting it higher so all could see its intricate veins. "It's from a tree that continues to grow and thrive regardless of the seasons. It reminds me of my own growth, especially during my recent divorce."

Lucas continued, his voice carrying a hint of vulnerability, "My divorce was a season of intense change and, at times, deep loneliness. But like this leaf, I've learned that growth can come from the most unexpected and challenging times."

He paused, looking down at the leaf, then back up at the group. "This leaf reached for the sun with every bit of its being. That's how I view my life now. I'm moving past the pain, growing from it, and finding new ways to connect and be present, both in my personal life and now here on this retreat."

Tina, visibly moved by his story, responded. "Lucas, thank you for that honesty. When you shared that, I got goosebumps. It's so awesome to see how you've connected your personal healing with the growth you're experiencing here."

Marina's enthusiasm filled the pavilion as she nodded approvingly. "Yes, yes! That's it!" she exclaimed. "This is how you forge deep connections. Notice how your responses focus not on your own experiences directly but on how you relate to and feel about what the other person is sharing?"

Her enthusiasm rising, "It's about creating a space where everyone feels seen and heard. When you respond in this way, you're actively participating in their process of expression. Who's next?"

Elizabeth stood, holding a piece of driftwood in her hands, her expression nostalgic. "This piece of driftwood represents a significant accomplishment in my life—

completing a triathlon against all odds." She paused, running her fingers over the smooth, weathered wood. "Just a year before the race, I was recovering from a serious knee injury. Many thought I wouldn't make it to the starting line, let alone the finish line."

She continued, "This piece of wood traveled great distances, tossed by seas, yet it emerged on shore, whole and beautiful. It reminds me of my own journey. To me, it symbolizes victory against the odds."

Brandon responded with a congratulatory tone; his eyes lit up with shared enthusiasm. "That's incredible, Elizabeth! Congratulations on such an achievement. As a surfer, I can totally relate to the feeling of overcoming the waves, both literal and metaphorical—it's exhilarating!"

Elizabeth nodded, her smile broadening with the sense of shared understanding. "Exactly," she replied. "It's about pushing through, no matter how rough the waters get."

It was clear that this exercise provided a lesson in the power of compassionate exchange and empathic listening.

After everyone had a chance to share their symbols and stories, Marina stood up and clapped her hands gently. "This," she said, "is the essence of what it means to bring your whole self to your practice. Each of you has shown professional acumen, personal courage, and relatability today."

She continued, "By listening to each other with such empathy and responding with resonance and respect, you've all demonstrated how your unique experiences and emotions can enrich your roles as coaches and leaders. This is about connecting human to human, heart to heart. *This* is how deep transformation happens."

Marina transitioned the group into an exercise designed to solidify the day's lesson. She instructed everyone to pair up with someone they hadn't worked closely with yet. The task was to discuss specific ways they could integrate their personal stories and unique attributes into their interactions without crossing the line of professionalism.

In pairs, participants engaged in thoughtful conversations. They explored scenarios where sharing personal insights, experiences, or emotions could enhance their professional relationships. They discussed boundaries to maintain professionalism while being authentic and transparent.

After ample time for discussion, Marina gathered everyone back into the circle for a debrief session. The pavilion buzzed with a renewed energy as each participant shared revelations and commitments they had made.

Tina spoke first. "Today has been an eye-opener for me," she began. "I've always known I'm pretty direct, and sometimes I've worried that it might be too much in my coaching sessions. But what I realized today is that my honesty could actually be a strength. It can help clients cut through their own excuses and really face what they need to. I just need to harness it correctly and make sure it comes from a place of empathy...which I don't do very well at the moment."

Brandon chimed in, "Man, I always try to tone down my humor in sessions, thinking it might not be 'professional' enough," using his fingers to air quote the word 'professional'. "But now I can see how my light-hearted approach could actually make clients feel more at ease. It might even break down barriers and make the tough parts of our sessions feel more relaxed and chill."

Marina nodded, pleased with their reflections. "Exactly, Tina and Brandon," she responded. "What you both bring to the table are your hidden treasures which are uniquely yours and can be incredibly effective in building trust and rapport. Tina, your hidden treasure is your honesty. When tempered with empathy, it can provide the clarity your clients need. And Brandon, your hidden treasure is humor, a tool that can lighten moments of heavy work, making the coaching process more enjoyable and less daunting."

Marina's encouragement resonated deeply, reinforcing the day's lesson about merging personal authenticity with professional techniques. The atmosphere was charged with a sense of empowerment as everyone contemplated how to weave their unique selves into their work.

Marina stood, her presence commanding attention as she prepared to conclude the session. "As we wrap up today, I invite you all to consider that coaching isn't just a question of technical skills. Yes, those are important, but the real magic happens in the human connection—the authentic interactions that enable those skills to have a greater impact."

She paced slowly, making eye contact with each participant. "Today, you've all seen firsthand how bringing your whole selves to your coaching conversations—your humor, your struggles, your triumphs—doesn't *detract* from your professionalism. Instead, it *enhances* it. Your hidden treasures make you more relatable, more trustworthy, and ultimately, more effective as coaches and leaders."

Marina continued, "They're what turns a good interaction into a potentially life-changing one. When you're genuine, you invite others to be genuine too. When you're open about your own experiences, you create a space for others to explore theirs. And that's where real growth happens."

She smiled, signaling the close of the session. "I invite you to carry this spirit of connection and authenticity forward into every interaction you have. You are all powerful catalysts for change. Thank you for embracing this journey so beautifully today." With that, she invited everyone to take a deep breath together, closing the circle with a collective sigh of release and achievement.

As Marina left the circle, the group broke into quiet conversations, pondering her words and mentally preparing to bring more of themselves into their coaching and leadership. The advice lifted a weight off many shoulders, offering permission to fully relax into their roles.

———————◆———————

Lucas made his way back to his yurt, the sounds of the retreat faded as he distanced himself from the pavilion. His mind was a whirlpool of thoughts. "Of course," he murmured to himself, "the more of ourselves we bring to the table, the more permission we give our clients to be fully authentic. It's about connection, not perfection."

His brow furrowed as he considered his own reservations, particularly about his divorce. He had always kept this part of his life shielded from his clients, worried that it might tarnish his professional image, make him appear less capable, or less deserving of their trust. "Have I been doing them a disservice?" he wondered silently. "By pretending everything in my life is flawless, am I inadvertently setting a standard that's alienating? Am I positioning myself above them instead of beside them?"

A flush of embarrassment rose as he considered the unintended barriers he might have built between himself and his clients. "This could change everything," he thought, his heart pounding with excitement. "Sharing my own struggles could dismantle this facade of perfection. It could foster a deeper, more genuine connection."

Resolved to embrace this new approach, Lucas entered his yurt and sat down with his journal to inscribe his commitment:

Today, I realized the true power of bringing my whole self to my coaching practice. In ways I seem to already do this well, like when I shared my emotional reaction with the craftsman yesterday. That felt very natural for me, and today Marina affirmed that we could do this to foster deeper connection.

But for too long, I've held back parts of my story, particularly my divorce, fearing judgment and doubting my own worthiness. But hiding these truths only distances me from my clients. From now on, I commit to being more open about my experiences—

not to overshadow my clients' journeys but to enrich our sessions with genuine empathy and understanding. I see now how sharing my vulnerabilities (or as Marina calls them, 'my hidden treasures') can actually strengthen trust and encourage my clients to embrace their own challenges with less fear. This isn't just about coaching; it's about human connection. Here's to breaking down walls and building bridges instead.

Lucas closed his journal and turned out the light. Tomorrow he would leave the island and be faced with putting all of these learnings into action. He knew the path ahead would require courage and adjustment, but he felt ready to see how this newfound openness would affect his coaching sessions, and also his relationship with himself.

Closing the Circle

On the final morning of the retreat, Lucas lay awake, his mind teeming with the wealth of knowledge he had gathered over the past week. Each lesson, each exercise was invaluable yet overwhelming in its depth. The excitement of applying these new skills was tinged with a thread of anxiety—how would he integrate all that he had learned into his coaching practice back home?

With a deep breath, he rose from his bed, showered, gathered his things, and headed out to join the others for their final breakfast on the island.

The group assembled in the open-air restaurant as the sun cast a warm glow over the ocean behind them. There was an energy of excitement about the journey ahead, yet there was a touch of melancholy, as the reality of leaving the island's serene sanctuary loomed.

Marina eagerly initiated a final sharing circle. "I'd love to hear from you," she began, "what are some of the biggest takeaways you're leaving the island with?"

The group exchanged thoughtful glances, each reflecting on the days packed with learning. Natalia was the first to speak up.

"I've redefined my value as a leader," Natalia shared, her voice confident. "Previously, I saw myself as a problem solver, a resource for others to depend on for solutions. But this retreat has shifted my perspective dramatically. I now see myself more as a mirror for others to find their own solutions and resources."

"That's a profound shift, Natalia," Marina responded. "It's essential for us as coaches and leaders to evolve our understanding of our role. Moving from being the solver of problems to being a facilitator of discovery empowers others in ways that are both deep and lasting. The master coach's value comes in their fine-tuned listening, their presence, and their whole-hearted belief in others."

She turned to address the whole group. "This redefinition of your value is crucial. It's about changing how you see yourselves and, consequently, how others see their own potential and power."

The group nodded, inspired by Natalia's insight and Marina's affirmation. "The best thing you can offer someone," concluded Marina, "is the insight to see—and solve—their challenges through their own capabilities. Thank you, Natalia. Who else wants to share?"

Tina eagerly jumped into the conversation. "I think the biggest discovery for me is that I've been working way too hard," Tina confessed. "What we learned here this week makes my job as a coach much easier. It's less about doing and more about just being. Also, using reflection more and not feeling like we always have to come up with a brilliant question, ya know?"

Tina paused, looking around as nods of agreement spread through the group. "What I'm taking away is letting the client do more of the work. It's obvious that they have all the best answers."

Marina responded with an encouraging smile. "Exactly, Tina," she said. "Masterful coaches trust in the client's ability and let them do the heavy lifting. Doing the work for them might feel generous and helpful but can also be disempowering to the client, making them feel inept, or like they need your help to arrive. This couldn't be farther from the truth."

She continued, "Our role isn't to provide answers but to guide others in discovering their own. This approach fosters their independence and builds confidence in their ability to handle challenges. Thanks, Tina."

Brandon chimed in next with his distinctive enthusiasm, "Coaching is even more awesome than I thought, and an incredible gift that we bring to our clients. Now I know why we get paid the big bucks!"

Marina, nodding in agreement, seized the opportunity to deepen the insight. "Absolutely, Brandon," she began. "Consider this—no one in your client's entire world will believe in them more than you. No one will listen to them as intently, be as curious about them, or empathize with them like you do. That is what makes you special."

She paused to let that idea sink in. "Your presence alone is invaluable, and you must never take it for granted. Whenever you leave a coaching conversation wondering if you did a good job, ask yourself: Were you 100% present with the person? Did you demonstrate an unconditional belief in them? Were you curious about who they are and what makes them tick? Did you listen with your heart, mind, and body? If you did those things, then you have truly earned your keep."

The group reflected on the responsibility and privilege that came with their roles as coaches and leaders.

As the conversation continued, each additional takeaway sparked a commitment to honor their unique position and their value.

Marina offered congratulations and a warm smile. "I'm proud of all you've accomplished this week. How is everyone feeling about taking these lessons back home?"

Lucas, feeling an urge to share his underlying concern, spoke up. "Marina, I've been thinking about everything we've covered, and while I'm excited to have learned so much here, I'm also a bit overwhelmed about integrating it all into my practice."

Marina responded with a reassuring tone. "It's completely normal to feel that way, but becoming a masterful coach is a marathon, not a sprint. You don't have to implement everything all at once."

Lucas replied, "You're right. Thank you for that. I just want to make sure I don't lose any of this momentum."

"Give yourself space and grace," Marina advised. "Rome wasn't built in a day, and neither were masterful coaches. Trust that the seeds of learning planted here will grow at their own pace. Your commitment to growth is evident, and it will guide you as you adapt these practices in your own time."

Elizabeth chimed in: "I guess it's about trusting the process, isn't it? Trusting that we'll know when and how to use what we've learned here."

"Exactly," Marina affirmed, "let these insights simmer within you. They'll find their way into your coaching naturally, as long as you keep your heart and mind open. You're not alone in this—you have a whole community of fellow coaches who are on similar paths. Lean on that, and remember, every small step is a part of your evolution."

The group's mood lightened, and Lucas felt a greater level of patience with himself and the process.

Natalia spoke up, "I think we should try to keep in mind that perfection isn't the goal—growth is."

"Well said, Natalia." Marina affirmed.

Marina turned her attention to the group, "As you move forward, stay open to all the transformations that will continue to unfold. Trust in yourselves and in the coaching process. You are all already exceptional professionals, so what you've learned here will enrich your toolkit, not replace it. And always, *always* stay curious. As Isaac used to say, 'We are only as wise as we are curious.' Embrace that curiosity, and let it be your guide."

With this mention of Isaac, Lucas felt a lingering question tug at him. He raised his hand and asked, "Marina, what ever happened to Isaac?"

Marina sighed deeply. "I wish I knew," she began. "When I returned to the island to set up this retreat, I searched everywhere for him. His cabin was just as I remembered it, but Isaac was nowhere to be found. I asked around the island, hoping someone might know something. But no one knew a man named Isaac. No one had ever even seen him." Her words hung in the air as the group absorbed the mystery.

"I couldn't make sense of it," she confessed. "Isaac was as real to me as any person I've ever known. His presence, his wisdom—it was all so tangible." She took a deep breath. "But over time, I realized that regardless of the mystery surrounding him, the wisdom he imparted was real. It transformed my life, and it guided the creation of this retreat. I'm grateful for every lesson learned, no matter how unexplainable it may seem now."

Marina's gaze swept across the group. "The essence of what you've learned isn't bound by the physical presence of any one person—it lives through the impact you have on others and through the wisdom you pass along. So, I encourage all of you, as you leave this island and return to your lives, to share the lessons with those you lead, mentor, and coach."

Her voice grew more passionate as she lifted her glass of freshly squeezed juice, "Let's honor Isaac's legacy by continuing to spread these insights. In this way, we keep his teachings alive, and they continue to guide us, no matter where we are or what we do."

After this inspiring toast, the participants joined hands for a closing ritual, each stating a word or phrase that captured their feelings or hopes for the future. Words like "growth," "connection," "empathy," and "courage" floated through the air.

As they parted ways, exchanging contact details and embracing warmly, the air was thick with promises to stay connected. The retreat may have ended, but the impact of their shared experience was just starting to unfold.

The Journey Begins

Lucas dragged his suitcase behind him as he made his way through the bustling airport, each step reflective of the past week. He settled into his seat on the plane, the familiar hum of the engines and the chatter of fellow passengers fading into a backdrop for his introspective mood.

As the plane ascended, Lucas pressed his forehead against the cool window, watching as the clouds enveloped the aircraft. The retreat, now a collection of vivid memories, had ignited a fire within him, and as the plane soared through the sky, so did his spirits.

He flipped to a new page in his journal to capture the flood of ideas and aspirations now racing through his mind. The workshops, the heartfelt conversations, the moments of quiet reflection by the sea—all were catalysts, propelling him towards a greater understanding of himself and his role as a coach.

As the plane rose above the clouds, Lucas's thoughts soared to the possibilities that lay ahead. He visualized the faces of clients, both current and future, and the deep connections he would forge through his enhanced approach. The retreat had recharged his passion for coaching and reminded him of its powerful impact on lives.

With the island now just a memory below the clouds, Lucas felt a renewed sense of commitment wash over him. He knew the road ahead would be challenging, but he felt invigorated, armed with new tools, fresh insights, and a rekindled spirit. The retreat had served as a pivotal platform for personal growth which allowed him to shed old fears and embrace new possibilities.

As the plane reached cruising altitude and the world unfolded beneath him, Lucas found himself brimming with anticipation. He was eager to explore the vast landscape of human potential, confident that this new chapter would be filled with discoveries, achievements, and the fulfillment of long-held dreams.

ABOUT THE AUTHOR

Jennifer Powers, MA, is an ICF Master Certified Coach and bestselling author. Since 2007, she has mentored thousands of coaches, created numerous ICF-accredited educational programs, and published *The Powerhouse Guide to ACC, PCC, and MCC Coaching*.

In an effort to support coaches to be their best, Jennifer founded Powerhouse Coaching, an international coaching school dedicated to developing the best coaches in the world. The school's highly rated ICF Accredited programs are designed to help coaches earn their ICF credential and coach at the absolute highest level.

Visit **www.phcoach.com** to learn more.

The Coaching Odyssey
At a Glance

DAY 1 – Harvesting Belief

Believe in others more than yourself. Trust that others are whole and resourceful enough to find their own answers. They just need your help to access them.

Remember, your belief in others could ignite others' belief in themselves.

DAY 2 – Unearthing Gems

Inquire more about the BEING than the DOING. Be genuinely curious about people's feelings, values, strengths, fears—rather than just the possible actions they can take or plans they can make.

Remember, what's happening on the inside inevitably shapes one's external realities.

DAY 3 – A Quiet Clearing

Practice embracing silence. Find moments to be silent with yourself and others. Notice how this practice affects your state of being, your interactions, and the space it creates for awareness to emerge.

Remember, silence is not something to be filled or avoided but embraced as a sacred space where true awareness can surface.

DAY 4 – Echo Valley

Use reflection as a powerful tool to build awareness. Reflection serves to mirror the person's beliefs, words, and emotions, and gives them space to be present with their value. Remember, questions like: 'Does that sound accurate?', 'What comes up for you as you hear that?', and 'How does that feel?' invite people to engage deeply and check in.

DAY 5 – Beyond the Rain

Practice multiple levels of listening. Tune into the entirety of what's being communicated—not only to what is in the forefront, but also to what might be in the background. Listen with your ears, your eyes, and your heart. Remember, sometimes the loudest truths are those unvoiced.

DAY 6 – Hidden Treasures

Consider integrating your personality, intuition, empathy, and humanity into the coaching process. Step back and let others navigate their path while bringing your whole self to the process.

Remember, the true art of connection lies not only in the techniques we employ when we engage others, but in the authenticity and heart we bring to each interaction.

Other books by Jennifer Powers available on Amazon:

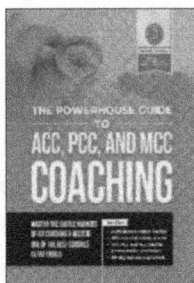

This cutting-edge guide gives you everything you need to master the art of ICF coaching. *The Powerhouse Guide to ACC, PCC, and MCC Coaching* is an essential resource for every coach, mentor, and trainer!

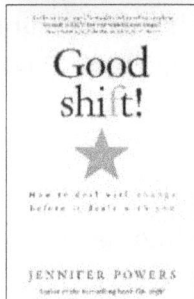

Jennifer brings her trademark wit and candor to shed light on the critical importance of embracing change. *Good Shift!* will help you (and your team) deal with change before it deals with you.

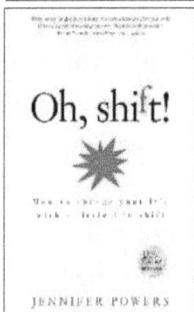

Break free from mediocrity and exercise your power of choice to live your best life. *Oh, shift!* is not only a great read for you but makes a perfect gift for your clients too!

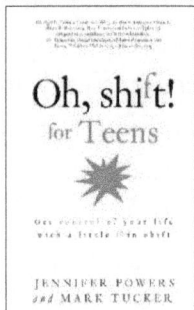

An easy-to-read, witty, and fun book that empowers teens to obtain independence, confidence, and better relationships. *Oh, shift! for Teens* places the power back into their hands.

www.ingramcontent.com/pod-product-compliance
Lightning Source LLC
Chambersburg PA
CBHW022340280326
41934CB00006B/706